We're
*All**M**ESSE**d*
UP

We're All Messed Up

WHY WE ARE AND HOW

GOD CAN CHANGE US

R. L. MITSCHELEN

Unless otherwise noted, all Scripture quotations are taken from the HOLY BIBLE, NEW INTERNATIONAL VERSION. Copyright © 1973, 1978, 1984 by International Bible Society.

All emphasis in Scripture quotations added by author.

ISBN: 978-1-7335526-0-8 (Paperback)
ISBN: 978-1-7335526-1-5 (E-book)

Front cover image by Pattadis / stock.adobe.com
Editing by Mary Freel
Book design by Jordan Mitschelen

First printing edition 2019.

"Most Christians expect little from God, ask little, and therefore receive little, and are content with little."

A.W. Pink (1886–1952)

Table of Contents

PHASE 1: ADMITTING YOU ARE UNHEALTHY

Self-Awareness Is the Frist Step to Health

INTRODUCTION

W e're all messed up. Me, you, your parents, your pastor, the pope, and the president are all messed up. Yes, some are more emotionally healthy than others, but we are all, to some degree, dysfunctional in some way.

So how can we determine if we are messed up? Here are just a few examples:

- We allow our circumstances in life to dictate our feelings instead of being content in all circumstances.
- We are afraid to share the truth about our sins and dysfunctions with others.
- We avoid confrontation.
- We over-react in certain situations.
- We have a deep sense that we're not as strong, mature, or emotionally healthy as we should be.
- We find ways to hide our faults.
- We look for ways to help pacify our negative emotions, insecurities, and pain.
- We react defensively to correction instead of admitting we're wrong and apologizing for what we've done.
- We are afraid to spend time alone in silence to reflect, pray and repent, and relinquish our control over our lives to God.
- We have some sort of emotional pain from a past experience that has never gone away.

Deep down, we all know we're unhealthy, but are afraid to admit it. If you don't believe me, look at these sobering statistics:

- 9.4% of Americans ages 12 and older use illicit drugs.[1]

- 11% of adults were prescribed anti-depressants in 2012 (over 29 million people), which includes 23% of women between the ages of 40–59.[2]
- 85% of young men and nearly 50% of young women reportedly watch porn at least once a month.[3]
- 1 in 3 American adults are food-addicted (clinically obese) in the U.S.[4]

- In New York, 1 in 5 preteens (children aged 6–12) have been medically diagnosed with ADHD, anxiety, bipolar disorder, or depression.[5]
- 1 in 10 girls reportedly engage in self-harm in the form of "cutting."[6]
- 1/3 of our nation's employees suffer from chronic debilitating stress,[7] and more than 1/2 of all "millennials" (18–33-year-olds) experience a level of stress that keeps them awake at night, including large numbers diagnosed with depression or anxiety disorder.[8]
- 28% of American adults have a drinking problem.[9]
- 1 in 3 women in the United States report experiencing some form of violence at the hands of an intimate partner at some point in her life.[10]
- Suicide is the 2nd leading cause of death of young persons aged 15–24.[11]
- Every day approximately 105 Americans die by suicide.[12]
- 100 million of us Americans are dependent on one toxic substance or another, legal or illegal, just to get through life.[13]

*Notes at end of book.

**(Go to Appendix A: Addictions
for more than 10 pages of statistics)**

Most, if not all, of these statistics continue to rise each year. This should make us take a long look at ourselves and realize that we are not addressing or healing our inner pain appropriately. Even if you are not included in any of the statistics above, chances are you still have emotional pain of some sort that has never been healed. We need to face the fact that almost all of us have issues that we haven't dealt with that are not going away regardless of what medications we take, or how many times we complain about our past hurts to others, or how much we try to suppress them by other means. The popular saying "time heals all wounds" is simply a lie. Our pain may become less intense over time, but it doesn't just go away. Unless we acknowledge that we are all dysfunctional and do the work needed to heal these inner wounds, we—our family, our friends, and our society—will continue to become worse.

One of the best methods I have found to help motivate myself to make healthy changes in my life is looking at the benefits that I would experience if I chose to make those changes. Getting emotionally healthy may seem a little vague as to why it may be important, so I think it's best to use the analogy of getting physically healthy as to why we should put just as much energy and time into getting emotionally and spiritually healthy as well.

For an example, here are the reasons that I use to tell myself why it is important to become physically healthy:

- #1 reason: More energy. Having more energy allows me to do my job (and do life) better as a spouse, mother, and employee. I have more energy to cultivate relationships with those around me by going to more events, going to church, and spending more time with my spouse and friends.
- I spend less money on health care.
- I spend less time at the doctor's office.

- Chances are that I'll live longer and spend more time with my family and friends.

Here are the benefits that I use to tell myself why it is important to become emotionally and spiritually healthy:

- #1 reason: Less over-reacting. I over-react much less to things said to me or when I'm in a difficult situation—saving me from saying or doing things I'll regret later and from hurting those around me.
- I am able to have more patience with others and to allow others to share without feeling the need to interrupt. I have less of a desire to talk about myself.
- My dependence on God is strengthened and my desires are more aligned with His instead of on those around me.
- I have less of a desire to impress others with material possessions, my career, or sharing Biblical knowledge that I may have at Church.
- Through Christ, I'm more OK with getting to know who I really am. I no longer try to hide my faults or sins with others. I have less negative self-talk.
- I am more easy-going. When times change, I change with them more easily.
- Through Christ, I am less controlling.
- I have a better sense of humor, and I'm more OK with laughing at myself.
- I don't gossip as much as I had before or feel the need to put others down.
- I more enjoy experiencing God's creation and resting in His presence. I enjoy reaching out to God when I am alone and listening to His voice.

Let me assure you that I was at one time pretty messed up; and I still am to a large degree. I have grown in these areas not on my own accord, but ONLY because God has healed me in the many dark and painful areas of my life. There are still many areas I need to grow and mature in, but God continues to heal me.

Doesn't being emotionally and spiritually healthy sound enticing? If so, let's begin the journey to discover how God can heal us one step at a time.

In my life, I've had the most success at making healthy changes when I've incorporated small, easy changes over time. Several years ago, I read a couple books on weight loss by Bob Greene, including *The Best Life Diet* and *Make the Connection*, that focused on getting healthier by incorporating small changes over time. As we all know, weight loss doesn't just happen overnight, and it doesn't happen by adjusting just one area of our lives. To achieve true, healthy living we not only need to eat well and exercise, but also master portion control, resist that donut at the office, add steps into our day, have accountability with another person, and be willing to change many other areas of our lives. I liked how I only had to work on a few areas at a time and make small changes little by little. This made the healthy changes that I had been making easier to stick with. Once I felt that I had succeeded in one phase, I could move on to the next. By the time I completed all three phases I had indeed become healthier and had lost weight. I've since realized that these healthy habits need to be continued through the rest of my life.

By implementing one area of foundational Christian truth at a time, letting go of the hurts, fears, and lies we've come to believe, and then using those same areas to heal the hurts of others, we can all become more emotionally healthy one small step at a time.

Just as in these weight loss books, we'll walk through several phases, not in the pursuit of physical wellness but of spiritual and emotional. We'll be using the acronym A.L.L.O.W. to help us remember each phase outlined in this book.

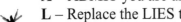

A – ADMIT you are unhealthy.
L – Replace the LIES that you believe with God's truth.
L – LET go of your past, your sins and your hurt.
O – Allow God the OPPORTUNITY to heal you.
W – Impact the WORLD by helping others to find healing.

When we A.L.L.O.W. God to come along side our emotional pain and begin to heal us, He can do truly remarkable things. Here is a brief outline of each phase:

During Phase one, we'll begin by admitting we are unhealthy. I know this may seem obvious, but sometimes it isn't. Sometimes, we want to remain exactly as we are and don't realize our need for emotional healing. We can become caught up in the actions of others and pinpoint the faults of those around us when we are the ones who need the most changing. As people of God, we can only become healthier by looking at ourselves, because we are the only part of the equation we can control. Once we admit that we are unhealthy, we can learn how we initially became unhealthy and what happens when we don't let go of pain. We'll learn how the devil works so we can defeat him in our thought life.

During phase two we'll replace the lies we've encountered with God's truth. We do this by memorizing scriptures that speak specific areas of doubt. We'll learn how knowing the depth of God's love can impact how we look at ourselves and those around us. Next, we will study each of God's inherent characteristics and change our view of God and his ability to heal us. At the end of phase one we'll learn how to take every thought captive, including our temptations. By building faith in both areas, we will be fully prepared to enter Phase three.

Phase three starts the healing process, first by letting go of our worries, fears, anxieties, and anything else that is inhibiting us from moving forward. Then we will learn about the power of prayer and why it is so important to our emotional and spiritual health. We will confess our sins to God, aligning ourselves with Him about our faults and mistakes, and learn about generational sin.

The fourth phase is when we release all our grievances to God by examining the hurts that we still hold onto, or any other hurts God might reveal to us. In surrendering our pain to God, He can show us the lies we believe by providing truth to replace them. We will list the ways Americans try to escape, and how they are unhealthy, as well as how to begin repairing our marriages. After we have received initial healing, we'll then set up an "emotional healthy calendar" so that we can continue the process of becoming emotionally healthy throughout our lives.

Once we have begun healing, we can begin phase five by discovering what God has called us to so we can begin to heal our community and impact our world. We'll learn how to reach out to others who are hurting and begin to heal our community by sharing testimonies of how God healed us; and reaching out to the children around us. In our faith we can begin the restoration of our churches, communities, and eventually the world.

CHAPTER 1 | 40 POUNDS OF POO

(WHAT HAPPENS WHEN WE DON'T LET GO OF PAIN)

A few years ago, my family and I went on a cruise where I attended a workshop on detoxing your body and weight loss (essentially a sales pitch for health products). To describe the importance of detoxing your body, the instructor mentioned that the famous western movie actor John Wayne died of stomach cancer. However, during his autopsy they discovered more than forty pounds of toxins (poo) in his colon. I just can't get that disgusting image out of my mind. Every time I hear John Wayne's name, his poo in his colon is what I think of. Pretty gross, huh? You probably never realized that we are all living like John Wayne...we all are carrying around a bunch of poo. Not literal poo (hopefully), but we carry a pile of hurts, fears, sins and grief that we've accumulated over the years. With every harsh word that's been spoken to us, every hurt that we've held onto, every sin that we've committed without repenting, and every lie that we've believed piles up. After time there's a weight that we have held onto that we so desperately want to and need to let go of.

Perhaps you've read your bible, had people pray for you, prayed for yourself, and talked to others about your "poo" (hurts, sins and fears). You've gone to church for years but haven't quite found an opportunity or a safe place to reveal this "poo" to others while still feeling completely loved and accepted. You believe that Christ can heal you but just haven't quite experienced a permanent healing. But if you don't receive healing at church, where else can you? Isn't that what the church is meant to be—a place for all to come and be healed? As the author John Ortberg said in a recent sermon he gave entitled "Nobody's Perfect" "Healing comes when you are fully known. Sickness remains when you hide… It's only when you are fully known, that you can be fully loved… We are not a community of perfect people, but are the mess-ups, the guilty, the betrayers, the failures, the sinners, the greedy, the sex-obsessed, etc…"[1]

Doesn't that sound refreshing, to know that we can truly be ourselves, load of poo and all, and that the church can potentially be that place where we are still fully loved and accepted?

I have recently found a community of believers where there's a potential for its congregation to be truly known and accepted. However, most churches I have attended over the years did not provide that place of openness. After many years of struggling with pain from my childhood, I had gone to my pastor wishing for him to help me. I was hurt and surprised when he didn't want me to share my history of pain with him. Because this pastor needed inner healing as well, he couldn't see his own hurt or have been able to address mine. At that time my pastor was overwhelmed with the physical needs of the church and suffered from depression. Eventually my pastor became burned out and had a moral failure that devastated many people, especially his family whom I dearly loved. I loved and respected my pastor and knew that if this could happen to him (who really was a great, godly and loving man), it could happen to anyone, (myself included) if we fail to confront and heal our inner pain. Once I started to receive inner healing from Christ, I realized that this is what had been missing in my Christian experience and it changed my life. I only wish I would have experienced this healing much earlier and that my former pastor could have experienced it as well.

But instead we've become skilled at hiding our hurts—especially at church. We want others to see us as competent, successful, faithful followers of Christ. But the problem is… we aren't. All of us, if we're honest, still have issues with people that hurt us in the past. We struggle with sin each day; we are hindered by fear. So we build unhealthy habits to compensate for the pain—usually without realizing it. We find things to do that dull our pain and offer some escape; either by working too much, taking unnecessary medication, looking at pornography, watching too much television, spending too much time on our phones and computers, or by eating too much. The statistics are very high for abuse in each of these areas, even among Christians. But, as long as we look good on the outside, everything is ok! Or is it?

I carried emotional pain for many years and never addressed it. Every time I'd think of my parents' divorce, I wanted to cry. I couldn't understand why this part of my past was still affecting me. So, to avoid feeling the pain, I wouldn't allow myself to feel or show that I was affected by the hurt within me and suppressed it deep inside for many years. It saddens me to think I was actively involved in the church as a youth leader for ten years, yet there was no opportunity for healing. My husband and I loved our church dearly and learned a great deal while we were there, but there was no event or opportunity to share the pain, or the dark things that were really going on in our home. I think there are many churches like that. The church is usually willing and able to pray for a job, for healing from sickness, and for others to be saved, but how often do we pray for someone struggling with depression, anxiety, or loneliness? How often do we actually confess our sins to others and ask for help to stop sinning? Even if you are catholic and go to confession, we usually don't ask for help or confess our sins to a friend. In my experience, protestants usually don't confess to anyone, let alone ask for help.

Christian counselor and successful author Larry Crabb states in his book *Encouragement*:

> The more I understand people and their needs, the more I am persuaded that God has uniquely designed the local church to respond to those needs. And as my conviction grows, so does my frustration.
>
> The needs of people, to at least some degree, are obvious to all but the most insensitive and self-centered. Even a causal consideration of the healing potential of relationship with Christ makes it clear that the deep wounds of hurting people can be substantially healed. But still we attend to lesser matters and lose sight of what can be done. The church, where Christ's holiness and love are to be evidenced the most, too often becomes an organization just seeking to perpetuate itself, while the reasons why it should continue and grow are obscured.[2]

So, how did we get this way? I have my own theory. When Adam and Eve were created, they could talk directly with God and go to Him for any advice they needed. Perhaps Adam did this to find out how to cultivate crops or how to take care of the animals. But when the serpent came to deceive Eve, she chose to go to Adam with whom she shared her forbidden apple. She could have chosen to ask God what He thought of the serpent's plan and receive His advice, but she chose not to because she wanted the knowledge of good and evil for herself and her husband. Since then, we have had the tendency (or temptation) to not take advice from others, pastors or priests, and especially from God, as our families have become exceedingly dysfunctional and as our faith in God has diminished over the years. Then later, as professional counselors came into place, we began choosing to go to a counselor, psychiatrist, or psychologist for help, replacing God and the family, friends and ministers that had surrounded us before. Although I do think there are times when going to a psychiatrist or psychologist is warranted, I believe it should be one of our last options, especially since these professionals tend to prescribe powerful medications that can have serious side effects, and in some cases make the situation worse. We should instead begin by going to God first and believe that He can heal us. Too often, this order has been reversed, and we are suffering the consequences of it today.

I also think that a son or daughter going to his or her parents, or a husband or wife going to his or her spouse or friend for advice should be natural. So it's important for us all to learn how to counsel others effectively, instead of us just complaining to each other about our problems, which really only makes the matter worse (something we will touch on in phase three). I do believe God can and does speak to us through emotionally and spiritually healthy people surrounding us, because they know us best and usually have our best interest in mind. However, because our friends, family and ministers may fail at times and give poor advice, and because families have become more and more dysfunctional, it is especially important to receive counsel from God throughout our lives. He is the only one who knows every aspect about you, who loves you unconditionally, and who knows the future and what action you should take next. The more people I speak to about counseling, the less I hear of any intention of seeking God, the true healer, for advice or healing. He should be where we turn first. God has given plenty of instruction in His Word regarding counseling and just how important it is. Faith-filled followers of Christ throughout the centuries have learned where and how to receive counseling from the Bible, which we have somehow forgotten over time:

How God, Holy Spirit and His Word counsels us:

- I will instruct you and teach you in the way you should go; and I will counsel you and watch over you (Psalm 32:8).
- Trust in the Lord with all your heart and lean not on your own understanding; in all your ways acknowledge Him, and He will make your paths straight (Prov. 3:5–6).
- All scripture is God-breathed and is useful for teaching, rebuking, correcting and training in righteousness, so that the man of God may be thoroughly equipped for every good work (2 Tim. 3:16–17).
- Cast all your anxiety on Him because He cares for you. (1 Peter 5:7).
- For the word of God is living and active. Sharper than any double-edged sword, it penetrates even to dividing soul and spirit, joints and marrow; it judges the thoughts and attitudes of the heart (Heb. 4:12).

- But the Counselor, the Holy Spirit, whom the Father will send in my name, will teach you all things and will remind you of everything I have said to you (John 14:26).

How we are to counsel each other:
- Therefore encourage one another and build each other up, just as in fact you are doing. (1 Thes. 5:11).
- Carry each other's burdens, and in this way you will fulfill the law of Christ (Gal. 6:2).
- Perfume and incense bring joy to the heart, and the pleasantness of one's friend springs from earnest counsel (Prov. 27:9).
- I myself am convinced, my brothers, that you yourselves are full of goodness, complete in knowledge and competent to instruct one another (Romans 15:14).
- The way of a fool seems right to him, but a wise man listens to advice (Prov. 12:15).
- Plans fail for lack of counsel, but with many advisers they succeed (Prov. 15:22).

To even better understand why we have turned away from God for advice, I think it's important to learn the history of counseling and how we have arrived to where we are today. So let's take a look back and walk through some of the major developments that have taken place.

A Brief History of Counseling & a Few Words on Antidepressants

It wasn't until the industrial revolution during the 18th and 19th centuries that we began going to professionals for counseling. Before then, we went to our family, a friend, a community elder or church leader, or to God for advice. This worked pretty well for centuries. But as people began moving towards inner cities seeking employment, they became separated from the emotional and spiritual support of their families and church. They could, however, still seek counsel from their now local church. But then a shift occurred. Many new professions came from the industrial revolution, including many professions within the field of science. Charles Darwin, who was famous for his contribution to the theory of evolution, wrote his first book, *On the Origin of Species* in 1859. It sold out the first day it was released. It has since become one of the most controversial books of the past millennium, and that work has since made Darwin the patron saint of modern atheism. According to Richard Dawkins in *The Blind Watchmaker*, "Darwin made it possible to be an intellectually fulfilled atheist."[3] Although this was never Darwin's intention, since he himself was agnostic (a person who claims neither faith nor disbelief in God) and was married to a devout Christian. Christians today do not have a problem with the concepts of natural selection (within its own kind) nor with survival of the fittest, but only of the theory of how the universe and how life began and the time it took, which was not developed by Darwin. Dating techniques were not developed until the 20th century, so Darwin did not have any concept of the time span now known to be involved.

At first Darwin's book was ignored by many of the Christian scientists of the day. The prevailing theology was natural theology—using science to prove God. But it was, in fact, Robert Chambers' book, who published earlier in 1844 (*Vestiges of the*

Natural History of Creation), which introduced progressive geology and evolutionary biology that provided a naturalistic explanation for the origin of the earth and the evolution of life, including man. This book set the tone for Darwin's work to become more acceptable during his time. Even with Chambers' book already published, Darwin recognized that his book would not receive a good response in a Christian culture and was concerned with how it would affect the Christian community. After Darwin's book was published, it was a man by the name of T. H. Huxley who used it to attack the Christian establishment and saw Darwinism as an explanation of creation, denying any role for a Creator.

> Charles Darwin would probably have only been a footnote to history if it had not been for the support given to him by the aggressively anti-Christian, Dr. Thomas Henry Huxley, MD. Dr. Huxley was nicknamed 'Darwin's Bulldog' [British, you know!] for his tenacious hatred of religion, Christians and creation. If it had not been for him dogmatically promoting Darwin we might not even think of the name.[4]

Throughout the years, his book did in fact influence many people, including Sigmund Freud. Sigmund Freud was an Austrian neurologist who developed psychoanalysis, a method through which an analyst unpacks unconscious conflicts base on the free associations, dreams and fantasies of the patient. His theories on child sexuality, libido and the ego, among other topics, were some of the most influential academic concepts of the

20th century. Even though his work has been both praised and highly critiqued, no one has influenced the science of psychology as Freud has. Being himself an atheist, he was one of the first to state that going to a priest or pastor was detrimental to one's emotional well-being. Instead, individuals were to seek counsel from a professional psychiatrist or psychologist. That is when the gradual shift began from people going to a local pastor for their spiritual and emotional guidance to going to a professional counselor who was not interested in their spiritual well-being began. At the beginning, people in this profession tried to unveil the reasons behind a person's emotional health, which included psychoanalysis, diving into the individual's past traumas. Through the years, these professionals then received the ability to prescribe medication. Over time, however, they began to prescribe these powerful medications much more frequently. So much so, that now, 11% of adults are prescribed anti-depressants, which includes 23% of women between the ages of 40–59.[5] 11% of children between the ages of 4 and 17 have been diagnosed with ADHD, who are also encouraged to take medication. That's an increase of 42% between 2003 and 2011.[6] This over-medication has created a society of people who no longer want to deal with inner pain and resolve to medicating it instead.

Today there are almost 300 "mental disorders" listed in the "psychiatric bible," or the DSM-5,[*] according to AllPhych. There are so many disorders now, it's been said that over half of the U.S. will have a diagnosable mental disorder in their lifetime. There are many mental disorders on this list that previously

---

[*] Standing for Diagnostic and Statistical Manual of Mental Disorders.

were not viewed as a "disorder" or "disease" in biblical times, but were viewed as a temptation, or a problem to struggle with, or a sin. The problem with this is when we label sins or problems we are facing as "mental disorders," we no longer see the problem as our fault. We look at it as a disease, as though we had no part in contributing to the problem we are facing. In an article titled "What Causes Mental Illness," Medicinenet stated, "Although the exact cause of mental illnesses are not known, it is becoming clear through research that many of these conditions are caused by a combination of genetic, biological, psychological, and environmental factors—not personal weakness or character defect—and recover from a mental illness is not simply a matter of will and self-discipline."[7] The problem with diagnosing these disorders is there are often no tests involved to verify if people really have these conditions. All counselors can go by are the symptoms the patient may be telling them they have. According to professional psychologists and psychiatrists, they label people with these mental disorders so they can then look up how other professionals may have treated the condition successfully in the past, as well as to have the treatment and prescriptions insured. I think the more likely reason is it gives them a reason to prescribe their patient more medications. The more mental disorders there are, the wider the market for medications to be prescribed. The DSM-5 and the pharmaceutical industry have a significant connection. One study found that 70% of the DSM-5 task force members have financial ties to the pharmaceutical industry. Pharmaceutical companies are making an enormous amount of money. In 2016, the industry generated 446 billion dollars.

Medical doctors are highly encouraged to prescribe medication for mental disorders. 65% of doctors have received kickback payments or gifts in the form of travel, research, gifts, speaking fees or meals from pharmaceutical or medical device companies.[8] Only 5% of their patients knew that they were given these incentives.

We can blame the dramatic increase in prescriptions for mental disorders (especially antidepressants) both on professional counselors and the patient alike. I was once told by a medical doctor friend of mine one day when I asked her the reason doctors prescribe so much medication, "It's because that's what people want. They want to walk away from the doctor's office with a quick fix for their problem." We no longer want to face the fact that our mental struggles might be our own fault and that we may need to make changes on our own to make ourselves healthier again.

Below is a partial list of mental disorders that I believe are not genetic or biological conditions, but are more closely derived from personal struggles, temptations or sin (that most likely stemmed from moments of inner pain):

Alcohol addiction, Amphetamine Addiction, Antisocial personality disorder, Avoidant Personality disorder, Caffeine Addiction *(I didn't know my need for tea in the morning was a mental disorder!)*, Cocaine related disorders, Computer Addiction, Disorder of Written Expression, Emotionally Unstable Personality Disorder, Female sexual disorder, Gambling Addiction, Hallucinogen Addiction, Hypoactive sexual desire disorder, Impulse control disorder, Inhalant Addiction, Insomnia, Intermittent Explosive disorder, Kleptomania, Language disorder, Male Sexual Disorder, Mathematics Disorder *(Really?)*, Morbid Jealousy, Narcissistic Personality disorder, Neglect of Child, Oppositional Defiant disorder, Paranoid Personality Disorder, Partner relational problem, Passive-aggressive personality disorder, Pathological gambling, Perfectionism, Personality disorder, Physical abuse, Post-traumatic embitterment disorder (PTED), Premenstrual Dysphoric Disorder (*Must have been a man who came up with that one!*), Pyromania, Reactive Attachment disorder, Relational Disorder, Sadistic personality disorder, Seasonal Affective disorder, Self-defeating personality disorder, and Sleep arousal disorder (along with many other disorders that I haven't mentioned).

Of course, I don't want to dismiss those with a clinical mental illness. There are many instances where proper professional treatment and medication is required. I am proposing, however, that we first investigate other areas of our life before we go to the doctor thinking we may need a prescribed medication. According to Prevention Magazine, there are 10 questions we should ask ourselves before we start taking antidepressants:

- Could my depression be the result of a medical condition?
- Could my depression be a side effect of another medication?
- Have a suffered a recent loss? (If so, go to the Chapter 10 on Grief to learn how to cope with the losses you've experienced)
- Am I exercising enough?

- Am I eating a healthy, well-balanced diet? A sugar-heavy diet can cause a severe drop in blood sugar levels, which can lead to feelings of low energy and depression. Additionally, gastrointestinal issues can lead to mood problems including depression.
- Am I socializing on a regular basis?
- Am I getting enough sleep?
- Have a tried to reduce my stress or anxiety?
- Am I drinking too much alcohol?
- Do I have a long-term plan for dealing with my depression?

Sometimes, no matter what you try—changing your diet, taking supplements, working with a therapist, or exercising—the darkness still looms; you may want to think about taking medication, especially if you find that the depression is inhibiting your daily functions," says Selhub. "So if you're seriously considering going on antidepressants, you should also have a plan for going off the meds, she says, and recommends weaning off antidepressants in 6 to 9 months after new coping habits have been formed—under the supervision of your doctor.[9]

I do want to emphasize that if you find that you can't get out of bed, or are having difficulty dealing with everyday life, then antidepressants may be what you need. Just be sure you aren't trying to avoid dealing with the emotional pain you may have. Remember, it's common to experience emotional pain in life, and God wants to help you through it. This book will show you how God can heal you of that pain. We'll begin the healing process in Phase 4.

One of the problems with prescribing antidepressant medication so prevalently are the side effects associated with antipsychotic and other strong medications. Some of the gentler side effects typically include nausea, vomiting, weight gain, diarrhea, sleepiness and sexual problems. Those sound bad enough, but there are also other side effects that have been shown, like thoughts about suicide, attempts to commit suicide, new or worsening depression, new or worsening anxiety, feeling very agitated or restless, panic attacks, insomnia, new or worsening irritability, acting aggressively, being angry or violent, acting on dangerous impulses, and extreme increase in activity and talking (mania). Relieving our pain shouldn't be as difficult, costly, or potentially harmful. God has a better way.

I recently watched a movie on Amazon Prime called *Letters from Generation RX*, directed by Kevin P. Miller. This movie documented several families whose lives were shattered from the effects of taking antidepressant medications. A couple of families had teenagers who committed suicide. Others were shown in court, describing what it was like being on antidepressants like Prozac, Zoloft and Paxil. One woman who pleaded in court asked, "Does a wonder drug make you forget a conscience? Does a wonder drug make you forget the difference between right and wrong?" Terence H. Young, whose daughter committed suicide, spent five years studying the practices of drug industries. He wrote a book called, *Death by Prescription*. He stated that prescriptions are now the 4th leading cause of death in our society. He also said that within nineteen seconds after a doctor enters a patient's room, he already knows which prescription he'll prescribe. I don't know about you, but nineteen seconds doesn't seem like a lot of time to sufficiently diagnose a patient!

The most heartbreaking part of the movie was observing two families whose fathers had murdered their own children. These men were at one time loving fathers, who would have done anything for their children, but when on antidepressant medication, were no longer able to distinguish reality from their irrational, disturbed thoughts.

They said the reason people begin to think irrationally on antidepressants is because in some cases, they can't break down the enzymes in the medication, causing the dosage within the blood to accumulate to where the patient becomes psychotic. They also stated that antidepressants can diminish frontal lobe activity, the part of the brain that tells someone when something is a bad idea.

These men were no longer able to distinguish between right and wrong and had an overwhelming sense of paranoia. One of the families they interviewed recounted how one mother, who was on antidepressants, drove herself and her four small children into a body of water, hoping they would all drown. Once in the water, she came to her senses and drove the car back out and the children were saved. However, she committed suicide a few years later and two of the children were diagnosed bipolar. The father, hoping desperately to save his children from the effects of bipolar their mother suffered, studied other ways of treating the disorder. He started giving his children high doses of micronutrients. Within months their symptoms diminished. After discovering such improvement from his children, he developed a company called TrueHope that sells supplements which incorporate micronutrients, vitamins and minerals that have had great success in treating those with ADD, ADHD, Anxiety, Autism, Bipolar, Depression, Fatigue, and Stress.

After watching the movie, I just sat and wept. The stories were so sad. They reminded me of a friend who also struggled with bipolar disorder and recently took his life. I saw how much he struggled when changing medications over the years. He could seem so emotionally healthy one moment, and a day later become manic. I just wish he wouldn't have had to suffer as he did. Perhaps he would still be alive today if he would have found a more natural, less invasive remedy.

I've read that periodic fasting can greatly improve one's mood and mental clarity. Some countries use fasting as a prescription for mental health and medical diseases and have had great success. There are many verses in the Bible that talk about fasting... not as a requirement, but as something common practice for spiritual direction, repenting and grieving. I think fasting can become an important part of our spiritual growth and help us experience deep reflection of our lives. I also believe preservatives and sugar influence our health in so many negative ways. By fasting and detoxing, we get rid of these chemicals within our body, and can experience greater mental and physical health. There are countless studies that show our diet is largely linked to depression. When many people have changed to a healthier diet, their signs of depression diminish. There are also many foods that exist which are known to help elevate our mood. The point is there are more natural solutions for depression and other mental disorders. Exercise, healthy eating, and healthy relationships with both God and others are all keys to living a more satisfying and productive life. We should constantly seek God's direction for steps to benefit our emotional, spiritual and physical well-being.

I also grieve over the many recent school shootings. I discovered that some 90% of school shootings for more than a decade have been linked to the same type of antidepressant, selective serotonin reuptake inhibitors (SSRIs), either while currently taking the medication, or while in withdraw from it, according to British psychiatrist Dr. David Healy, a founder of RxISK.org.[10]

In his book, *Signature Sins*, Michael Mangis, a psychologist, states, "[Psychotropic medications] are a tempting escape for those who do not want to do the difficult work of facing the pain and loss which caused the depression in the first place. Where depression and anxiety have become incapacitating, medication can free a person of enough symptoms that the person can face and tackle the wounds of the past. We should never use antidepressants as a magic escape to avoid the vital work of inner healing."[11]

I have read of an instance where a local pastor had encouraged a woman in his congregation to take an antidepressant in order to dull the pain in her life. Once on these medications, she was no longer able to feel true grief, nor true joy. She eventually left her church to join another congregation that encouraged her to not only feel her pain but also discussion with God and others within the congregation in order to heal.

If you are currently taking antidepressant medication and would like to be taken off, I would strongly recommend that you talk to your doctor as to how you can safely taper from the medication. Coming off these drugs can have harmful effects as well, so it's important to go do it the best way possible.

In Rev 18:23 it states, "The light of a lamp will not shine in you again. The voice of bridegroom and bride will never be heard in you again. Your merchants were the world's greatest men. By your *magic spell* all the nations were led astray" (NIV) (emphasis mine). Pharmakeia, which is the original Greek translation for sorcery and in this verse "magic spell," is also the word from which we developed the English words "pharmacy" and "Pharmaceutical." This verse implies that in the end times, nations will be deceived through the means of medications, drugs, and other methods of deception. Most bibles use the word sorcery in place of the word pharmakeia. Some of the synonyms for sorcery are "enchantment," "magic spell," and "entrancement." I believe that the over-use of medications used to treat depression has been one of the methods the devil has used to entrance us. If we become altered in our thinking in any way—either by taking medications, drugs, or alcohol, I believe it becomes more difficult to hear from the Holy Spirit. We also become more susceptible to the lies the devil wants us to believe.

I believe that these are all tactics the devil has used throughout the years to steer us away from genuinely healing our pain. If we are not healed, it affects our relationships (especially our marriages) and our overall well-being. He continues to lie to us, making us believe our struggles and temptations are not something we can control or gain victory over with God's help. He tries to convince us that time will eventually heal our wounds, or that we'll feel better if we complain about our problems. God wants so much more than that for you. He wants you to be whole; to be healed and to be healthy in all your relationships. He wants you to trust in Him. By better understanding the devil and his tactics, we will become better at defeating him. By better understanding God and His true character traits, we become better at trusting Him to heal our pain.

I.

CHAPTER 2 | CADDYSHACK

(UNDERSTANDING HOW THE DEVIL WORKS)

*For our struggle is not against flesh and blood,
but against the rulers, against the authorities,
against the powers of this dark world and against
the spiritual forces of evil in the heavenly realms
(Ephesians 6:12).*

*Be self-controlled and alert. Your enemy the devil
prowls around like a roaring lion looking for
someone to devour (1 Peter 5:8).*

Caddyshack is a 1980 American sports comedy film that has been hailed by media outlets, such as Time and ESPN, as one of the funniest sports movies of all time. The movie takes place at an upscale golf country club. Carl Spackler, one of the greenkeepers, is entrusted with the task of combatting a potentially disastrous gopher infestation. He tries a variety of methods to kill the gopher, like shooting and drowning, without success.

By the time two of the main characters in the movie reach the final hole in a competitive game of golf, the score is tied. At the climax of the game, the leading character, Danny, is about to attempt a difficult putt to win. At that moment, Carl, in his latest attempt to kill the gopher, detonates a series of plastic explosives that he has rigged around the golf course. The explosion shakes the ground and causes the ball to drop into the hole, handing

Danny the victory. The gopher emerges unharmed and dances amid the smoldering ruins of the golf course.

Even though I would not suggest viewing the entire R-rated movie, I would recommend watching this particular scene on YouTube, where Carl is talking through his plan to kill the gopher. He says to himself, "Licensed to kill gophers by the government of the United Nations. Man, free to kill gophers at will. To kill, you must know your enemy, and in this case my enemy is a varmint. And a varmint will never quit—ever. They're like the Viet Cong—Varmint Cong. So you have to fall back on superior intelligence and superior firepower. And that's all she wrote."

You see, Carl (as dysfunctional as he was) was able to discern that in order to defeat his enemy, he had to know his enemy, which in this case was a gopher. Like Carl, we need to know and understand our enemy as well, which in our case is the devil. And like this gopher, he will never quit trying to attack us. We must fall back on superior intelligence and superior firepower.

Understanding the devil and his schemes was a significant piece that was missing in my Christian walk. Throughout our years in church we learned about how loving our Father was, life lessons taken from bible events, and how to grow in our Christian walk; but we didn't learn about the devil and the methods he typically uses to attack us. If you don't know how the devil works, you can't defeat him. I realize now that this is a very important part of the healing process.

Here is a list of some of the characteristics of the devil that we can learn from Bible:

- Lies, and is the father of lies (John 8:44).
- Tempts people to sin (Matthew 4:1–11).
- Causes people to lose their faith (Romans 10:17).
- Created by God, but not equal to God. (Proverbs 16:4)
- Refuses to obey God and despises truth. (John 8:44)
- Was given limited power. (Job 1:8–12)
- Plans to steal, kill and destroy. (John 10:10)
- Rules the masses outside of God's protection. (Eph. 2:1–3)
- Tries to hide the actual truth about God. (2 Cor. 4:3–4)
- Twists Scriptures in our minds to fit his purposes. (Gen. 3:1–5)
- Will suffer the fate he deserves. (Revelation 20:10)

The most common way that the devil works today is through placing lies within our minds. If we don't take these lies (which we think are just our thoughts) captive and remove them with God's truth, these lies can then turn into beliefs that we then carry with us throughout our lives. In fact, every sin that we have committed began from lies that we have believed.

In his book *The Prodigal Prophet: Jonah and the Mystery of God's Mercy*, Tim Keller says, "All sin against God is grounded in a refusal to believe that God is more dedicated to our good, and more aware of what that is, than we are."[1] These lies are usually planted through an event, through continuous sin, or through generational sin.

My mind was full of self-defeating thoughts (lies), which kept me from growing in my Christian walk. I would always be thinking about how stupid, ugly, and fat I was and that no one really loved or liked me. During the first healing class I attended, called "Living Waters," I brought all of these self-defeating thoughts to God out loud, asking Him to remove them from my mind, while being surrounded by loving and supporting women. In this prayer, God placed in my mind the scripture Romans 8:1. "Therefore, there is now no condemnation for those who are in Christ Jesus." Immediately many of these troubling thoughts went away, and for the most part, have not come back.

I realized that the devil had been working in my thought life for years and had contributed to many of my hurts throughout my life. He is so much more powerful and evil than we think He is. He has fed you lies that you have believed, perhaps for most of your life. Until we recognize that we have fallen for these lies, we can't heal or grow in our faith in the areas in which those lies were implanted. If I believe I will always be fat, then no matter how many diets I'm on, or how much I exercise, I'll never be thin. If I believe I'll never have a great marriage, then we won't. If I believe that God doesn't love me, or is mad at me, when in fact He does love us and has never had a bad thought about us, then no matter how much God has blessed us, we won't see it. If I believe that my brokenness is not my fault, and that there's nothing I can do to heal, then I'll always be broken.

One of the biggest lies that we all share is that our brokenness is not our fault. But it is. Yes, others may have hurt us deeply, but it is our response to being hurt that is, more often than not, sinful. We repress, suppress, yell at those around us, pull away emotionally from God and from those around us, gossip and complain about our hurt to others, numb our pain by escaping in some way, or by denying that the pain is even there. These actions are all sinful, and we must begin to look at it that way. Larry Crabb has said, "Brokenness, isn't so much about how bad you've been hurt but how you've sinned in handling it."[2] He goes on to loosely quote Hosea 7:13–14, stating, "I long to redeem my people but they're not crying out for me! They wail upon their beds! They do nothing more than hurt over their circumstances." We need to begin to heal by replacing the lies we have believed with the truth about ourselves, about God's word and about God's character—and by calling out to God Himself!

PHASE ONE SUMMARY AND DISCUSSION QUESTIONS

PHASE ONE SUMMARY:

A = <u>Admitting</u> you are unhealthy

- We need to first admit that we are, in fact, messed up.
- We learned what happens when we don't let go of pain.
- By learning how we initially became unhealthy, we learned how to help us to avoid being unhealthy in the future.
- We learned how the devil works so that we can defeat him.

DISCUSSION QUESTIONS:

1. So, do you admit that you can grow more emotional healthy? If so, in what ways?

   ABSOLUTELY. I THINK I CONSUME A LOT OF THINGS THAT DAMAGE ME EMOTIONALLY

2. In what ways have you carried emotional pain in your life? How have you been trying to cope with that pain?

   I BELIEVE A LOT OF LIES ABOUT MYSELF AND WHEN I DO THAT, I DON'T BELIEVE WHAT GOD TELLS ME ABOUT ME.

3. Discuss ways in which our society has changed throughout the years by how we handle emotional pain.

   I THINK IT'S VERY ENCOURAGED FOR FEMALES TO HANDLE THEIR EMOTIONAL PAIN, IT'S NOT ENCOURAGED FOR GUYS TO DO THAT THO.

4. In what ways do you think the devil has been working in
) your thought life? When did this begin?

   HE LOVES TO TELL ME I DON'T HAVE
   WORTH. THIS BEGAN IN HIGHSCHOOL AND
   ITS MORE INTENSE IN COLLEGE.

5. Are you ready to do the work to become more emotionally healthy and begin phase two? If you are hesitant,
   why?

   IM WORRIED TO BRING ALL THESE
   THINGS TO THE SURFACE

PRAYER TIME:

If you believe that you need emotional healing, ask God to help guide you through this process of healing and to begin to open your eyes to some of the lies that you may have come to believe.

PHASE 2: REPLACING LIES WITH TRUTH

Replacing Junk-Food Lies with Nourishing Truth

CHAPTER 3 | COUNTERFEIT BILLS

(MEMORIZING SCRIPTURE)

D id you know that a large number of counterfeit bills are distributed through the bank? The very institution in which you put your trust has been deceived through the years by cycling counterfeit bills through their system unknowingly. How can this happen? This is made possible by the tellers who are not properly trained in detecting counterfeit bills.

Do you know how the FBI trains their employees to be able to detect a counterfeit bill? They learn not by studying examples of all the different types of counterfeit bills that have been identified, but by studying the real thing! They study those $1, $5, $20, and $100 bills for weeks and weeks until they know every detail of every bill. They study the bills so intently that they are able to detect a counterfeit within seconds.

We can apply this same strategy when detecting counterfeit thoughts. We can detect lies from the devil more easily when we can compare those thoughts with scripture and then discern whether those thoughts sound like they are coming from God, or from somewhere else. In my Christian walk, I always knew it was important to learn scripture, but I didn't fully understand WHY. I've since learned that memorizing verses from the Bible is essential in order to combat the lies that become implanted in our minds.

I used to have thoughts like "I'm stupid," "I'm fat," "No one cares about me"... Do any of these thoughts sound familiar?

These thoughts are not coming from God. In fact, **God has never had a bad thought about you** (in fact, you are the apple of God's eye! Psalm 17:8). These self-defeating thoughts are lies coming from Satan. We need to become aware of our negative thought life and replace them with God's truths before they continue to cause damage in our lives.

Take some time to look through this list of common lies we believe and consider if you have believed them as well. Then memorize the listed verses to use as your arsenal against the devil and any lies he tries to tell you. Let the truth of Scripture reassure you and redirect your thinking!

Some lies we typically believe about ourselves include:

No one understands what I'm going through.
> Jesus has been hurt as we have hurt, cried as we have cried, and has been tempted as we have been tempted (Matt. 27:46, Heb. 2:18, Heb. 4:15, Mark 3:5, John 11:33–34).

I'm worthless.
> As a child of God, I'm a fellow heir with Christ (Romans 8:15–17).

I'm alone.
> God will never leave you nor forsake you (Heb. 13:5).

I'm stupid.
> In Christ Jesus, I have wisdom (James 1:5).

No one loves me.
> I have been chosen of God and I am holy and loved (Col. 3:12).

I don't have any friends.
> I am a friend of Jesus (John 15:15).

I'm ugly or fat.
> My body is a temple of the Holy Spirit who dwells in me (1 Cor 6:19).

I'll always be this way.
> I'm a new creature in Christ (2 Cor. 5:17).

I'll never do anything with my life.

God created me to produce good works (Eph 2:10).

I'll never be able to support myself.

God supplies all my needs (Phil 4:19).

I'll never be content.

I will be content in all circumstances (Phil 4:12).

I'll never be good enough.

I have been set free from the law of sin and death (Romans 8:2).

I must be perfect.

"If we claim to be without sin, we deceive ourselves and the truth is not in us" (1 John 1:8).

I must have everyone's love and approval

"Am I now trying to win the approval of men, or of God? Or am I trying to please men?

If I were still trying to please men, I would not be a servant of Christ" (Gal 1:10).

It is easier to avoid problems than to face them

"Consider it pure joy, my brothers, whenever you face trials of many kinds, because you know that the testing of your faith develops perseverance. Perseverance must finish its work so that you may be mature and complete, not lacking anything" (James 1:2–4).

My unhappiness is someone else's fault.

"For we are each responsible for our own conduct" (Gal 6:5, NLT).

My worth is determined by my performance.

"I am fearfully and wonderfully made" (Psalm 139:13–14).

Life should be easy

"In this world you will have trouble" (John 16:33).

Life should be fair.

"Righteous men get what the wicked deserve, and wicked men who get what the righteous deserve" (Eccl 8:14, NIV).

People are basically good.

"There is no one righteous, not even one; there is none who understands, no one who seeks God" (Romans 3:10–11, ESV).

Some lies we typically believe about God include:

God's love must be earned.

For it is by grace you have been saved, through faith—and this is not from yourselves, it is the gift of God—not by works, so that no one can boast" (Eph. 2:8–9).

God hates people who sin.

"While we were still sinners, Christ died for us" (Rom 5:8).

Because I'm a Christian, God will protect me from pain and suffering.

In this world you will have trouble (Romans 5:3–5).

All my ailments are the result of sin.

"'Rabbi, who sinned, this man or his parents, that he was born blind?' 'Neither this man nor his parents sinned,' said Jesus, 'but this happened so that the work of God might be displayed in his life'" (John 9:2–3).

It is my Christian duty to meet all the needs of others.

"Now you are the body of Christ, and each one of you is a part of it. And in the church God has appointed first of all apostles, second prophets, third teachers, then workers of miracles, also those having gifts of healing, those able to help others, those of gifts of administration, and those speaking in different kinds of tongues. Are all apostles? Are all prophets? Are all teachers? Do all work miracles? Do all have gifts of healing? Do all speak in tongues? Do all interpret? But eagerly desire the greater gifts. And now I will show you the most excellent way" (1 Cor. 12:27–31).

Good Christians shouldn't feel angry, anxious, or depressed.

"Jesus wept" (John 11:35).

"My soul is overwhelmed with sorrow to the point of death" (Mark 14:34).

"In your anger do not sin" (Eph. 4:26).

God can't use me unless I'm spiritually strong.

"To the weak I became weak, to win the weak" (1 Cor. 9:22).

There is no such thing as stable truth.

"I am the LORD, I do not change" (Malachi 3:6, NKJV).

"Your statutes stand firm . . . O LORD" (Psalm 93:5, NIV).

"All His precepts are sure. They stand fast forever and ever" (Psalm 111:7, 8, NKJV).

"Your word is truth" (John 17:17, NKJV).

"The word of God . . . lives and abides forever" (1 Peter 1:23, NKJV).

"Heaven and earth will pass away, but My words will by no means pass away" (Matthew 24:35, NKJV).

"To the law and to the testimony! If they do not speak according to this word, it is because there is no light in them" (Isaiah 8:20, NKJV).

We should be skeptical of God, as He doesn't have good intentions.

"Taste and see that the Lord is good; blessed is the one who takes refuge in Him" (Psalm 34:8).

"You are good and do good; Teach me Your statutes" (Psalm 119:68).

God is boring and insignificant.

"Better is one day in your courts than a thousand elsewhere; I would rather be a doorkeeper in the house of my God than dwell in the tents of the wicked" (Psalm 84:10).

God must hate me.

"For God so loved the world, that He gave His only Son, that whoever believes in Him should not perish but have eternal life" (John 3:16).

"While we were still sinners, Christ died for us" (Romans 5:8).

God just wants you to be happy.

God does want you to be happy, however the Bible places more importance on having an everlasting joy by obeying the Lord, and not seeking happiness in the things of the world, since this happiness won't last. (Psalm 128:1-2) (Prov. 9:10), (Prov. 16:20) (Prov. 28:14) (Prov. 29:18)

Church is not important.

"Let us not give up meeting together, as some are in the habit of doing, but let us encourage one another—and all the more as you see the Day approaching" (Hebrews 10:25).

Following God's Word is too hard and you'll never have any fun.

"Cast your cares on the Lord and He will sustain you; He will never let the righteous fall" (Psalm 55:22).

"I delight greatly in the Lord; my soul rejoices in God. For He has clothed me with garments of salvation and arrayed me in a robe of righteousness, as a bridegroom adorns herself with her jewels" (Isaiah 61:10).

There won't be a Judgment Day.

"But I tell you that men will have to give account on the day of judgement for every careless word they have spoken" (Matt. 12:36).

You have plenty of time to choose to obey God.

"Therefore keep watch, because you do not know on what day your Lord will come. But understand this: If the owner of the house at what time of night the thief was coming, he would have kept watch and not let his house be broken into. So you must also be ready, because the Son of Man will come at an hour when you do not expect Him" (Matt. 24:42–44).

The Word of God is not true.

"Yet you are near, O Lord. And all your commandments are true" (Psalm 119:151).

Truth is relative (the opposite of absolute truth).

If all truth is relative, then that statement itself is relative as well—which means we can't trust it to be true all the time. Here are some verses that show that absolute truth is unchanging:

"God is unchanging" (Malachi 3:6); "Jesus likened His teachings to a solid, immovable rock" (Matthew 7:24). "Jesus is the only way of salvation, and this is absolutely true for every person at all times" (John 14:6). "Just like people need to breathe in order to live, people need to be born again through faith in Christ to experience spiritual life" (John 3:3).

There is no such thing as absolute truth.

"I the Lord do not change" (Malachi 3:6).

"Your statutes stand firm . . . O LORD" (Psalm 93:5).

"The works of His are faithful and just; all His precepts are trustworthy. They are steadfast for ever and ever" (Psalm 111:7-8).

"Your word is truth" (John 17:17, NKJV).

"The word of God . . . lives and abides forever" (1 Peter 1:23, NKJV).

"Heaven and earth will pass away, but my words will never pass away" (Matthew 24:35).

"To the law and to the testimony! If they do not speak according to this word, it is because there is no light in them" (Isaiah 8:20, NKJV).

God doesn't heal or perform miracles anymore.

God gave Paul and others the gift of performing miracles (Elijah, Elisha, Joshua, Moses and Aaron, Peter)

"God was performing extraordinary miracles by the hands of Paul" (Acts 19:11).

God gave some Christians today the gift of miracles: "… to another miraculous powers, to another distinguishing between spirits, to another speaking in different kinds of tongues, and to still another in the interpretation of tongues" (1 Cor. 12:10).

God is unapproachable.

"Come near to God, and He will come near to you" (James 4:8a).

God wants you to be perfect.

"There is not a righteous man on earth who does what is right and never sins" (Ecc. 7:20).

You don't matter to God.

"But, Brothers, whom the Lord loves, it is our duty always to thank God about you, for, from the first, God chose you for Salvation through the purifying influence of the Spirit, and your belief in the Truth" (2 Thess. 2:13, TCNT).

It's really important to recognize that these are all lies that Satan wants us to believe. **All of the bold statements are untrue.** We'll talk about just how much God loves us in Chapter 4. In Chapter 5, we'll be going over the each of the true character traits of God.

CHAPTER 4 | FULLY KNOWN AND FULLY LOVED

(KNOWING JUST HOW MUCH GOD LOVES US)

The most passionate presentation I have heard about God's love comes from Brennan Manning in his sermon entitled, "God loves you as you are, not as you should be." I would greatly encourage you to watch the video recording on YouTube. It's incredibly powerful. It's incredibly powerful because Brennan Manning has experienced the overwhelming love of God in his own life. In this video Manning shares the story of his own broken past and how God rescued him from himself by experiencing the love of God, even when he was at his worst (again, you HAVE to hear his story!). He states, "The next time you look at the cross, learn at what price you are loved. All God asks is that you marvel, be surprised, let your mouth hang open in silent wonder, and begin to breathe deeply… let the focus of your inner life rest on one truth. The staggering, mind-blowing truth that God loves you just as you are, and not as you should be, because no one in this building is as they should be. That God loves **you**, not the person next to you, not that God loves Billy Graham, or Mother Theresa, or that He loves the church or the world… but the truth that God loves you in such a way that He'd rather die, than be without you." He communicates that he's seen many Christians not believe this truth. He has seen many Christians live in fear, guilt, low self-esteem, remorse, self-condemnation, and self-hatred. Manning goes on to say, "Or they believe that God loves them in some vague, distant abstract way. But they'd be hard pressed to say that the essence of their Christian life is a love affair, a furious love affair that is going on between Christ and themselves at this very moment."

When Rich Mullins was alive, he heard one of Manning's messages on God's love on tape while driving to his next performance. When he began to listen to Manning's message, he was so moved that he had to pull over the car to the side of the road and weep. Even though this famous Christian artist had been performing for years singing about God, as well as teaching others about Him, He still didn't fully comprehend God's love for Him. He grew up with an abusive father and had never experienced the love and acceptance he so desperately desired. After his encounter with God on the side of the road, Mullins contacted Manning and they became great friends as Manning continued to help him grasp the concept of God's love for him.

I have always had the intellectual knowledge the God loved me, but I never truly experienced the incredible depth of God's love that He had for me until He healed me of my past pain. It was a transforming realization—that God would be so intimate with me and care for me so much that He would enter into the depths of my pain and take it away. He can do the same for you.

Here are some verses to help us be reminded of God's love for us:

John 3:16 - For God so loved the world, that He gave His one and only Son, that whoever believes in Him shall not perish but have eternal life.

Romans 8:37–39 - No, in all these things we are more than conquerors through Him who loved us. For I am convinced that neither death nor life, neither angels nor demons, neither the present nor the future, nor any powers, neither height nor depth, nor anything else in all creation, will be able to separate us from the love of God that is in Christ Jesus our Lord.

Ephesians 2:4–5 - But because of His great love for us, God, who is rich in mercy, made us alive with Christ, even when we were dead in transgressions, it is by grace you have been saved.

Romans 5:8 - But God shows His own love for us in this: While we were still sinners, Christ died for us.

Zephaniah 3:17 - The Lord your God is with you, He is mighty to save. He will take great delight in you, He will quiet you with His love, He will rejoice over you with singing.

1 Peter 5:6–7 - Humble yourselves, therefore, under God's mighty hand, that He may lift you up in due time. Cast all your anxiety on Him because he cares for you.

Psalm 86:15 - But you, O Lord, are a compassionate and gracious God, slow to anger, abounding in love and faithfulness.

CHAPTER 5 | BRUCE ALMIGHTY

(TRUSTING IN GOD'S CHARACTER)

O ne of our family's favorite movies is Universal Studio's *Bruce Almighty* (2003). The main character, Bruce Nolan (played by Jim Carrey), thinks that God is being unfair to him. He is a news reporter who keeps getting the worst stories to cover, doesn't get the promotion he wants, and thinks life is more difficult for him than for others.

When Bruce's frustration builds up, he grumbles, "God is a mean kid sitting on an anthill with a magnifying glass, and I'm the ant. He could fix my life in five minutes if He wanted to, but he'd rather burn off my feelers and watch me squirm." (You'll have to see the movie to see how God responded to his complaint!)

I think this quote best sums up what most people believe about God (if they were really honest). At one time, most Americans believed that God is all-powerful and all-knowing. They believed God is for the most part good. But over the last 50 years or so, society's perception of God has withgone a change that I personally believe has derived from the teaching of evolution in our public-school system.

Many people believe that if God really loved them, He would fix their lives (according to how they think their lives should be made "right"). In the last chapter we learned just how much God loves us. So, if God really loves us, wouldn't He or shouldn't He want to fix our lives? That's an honest question.

But I think once we begin to understand just who God is and what His natural character traits are, we would then begin the process of understanding God more fully and why things may not always work out the way we want them to.

Take a moment and write down all of the traits of God that come to your mind. Seriously, take out a pen and write. I'll wait... So, what did you come up with? What characteristics of God did you list? Now, I want you to take that piece of paper and throw it away. Really! We are starting from scratch today learning what the true characteristics of God are. Not the traits of God we've seen in movies, or the traits of God we've grown up believing, or the traits of God that someone else has told us, but the true traits of God as revealed in the Bible. I know this list seems a little long, but hang in there and please don't skip this part. Knowing God's attributes give us a new perspective of all that God is capable of and just how awesome He is. It is also so nourishing for our soul. When we really know and understand God's character, we'll know that we can go to Him for anything; especially with our pain, grief and sin. Ready? Let's begin!

God is Powerful

Today most colleges (even some Christian colleges) stress evolution as a fact. It just isn't. It's only a theory. Think about it; if the devil is able to convince us that God didn't really create the world in six days, then it significantly alters what we believe God is capable of doing. It makes us believe the Bible really isn't true, and that God really isn't as powerful as He says He is. I think this is where many people mess up their view of God. If you don't believe that God really created the world and everything in it in just six days, then that is a problem. I would encourage you to study Genesis chapters 1–9 to discover the true history of creation.

Romans 1:28, states, "Furthermore, since they did not think it worthwhile to retain the knowledge of God, He gave them over to a depraved mind, to do what ought not to be done." The "Believer's Bible Commentary" of the New Testament, offers a reason why so many people today believe in evolution, referencing Romans 1:28, which states, "This verse gives deep insight into why evolution has such enormous appeal for natural men. The reason lies not in their intellects but in their wills. They do not want to retain God in their knowledge. It is not that the evidence for evolution is so overwhelming that they are compelled to accept it; rather, it is because they want some explanation for origins that will eliminate God completely. They know that if there is a God, then they are morally responsible to Him."[1]

If this is an area where you have a problem believing, then I would recommend seriously studying the vast number of articles and videos produced by the Institute for Creation Research, Bible Discipleship Ministries, Apologetics Press, Creation Ministries International, Creation Today, David Rives Ministries, and Answers in Genesis (Curators of the Creation Museum and the Ark Encounter). Also visit the Genesis Science Network (which is a free digital channel, that streams like Netflix), as well as many other wonderful scientists that have shown time after time all of the supporting evidence for creation. It's just overwhelming, and there's just so much more evidence to support creation than what little evidence there is for evolution.

Once we come to believe that God did create everything in the world in six days, we can then begin to understand just how vast His power is. And if God can literally create something from nothing, He can certainly heal our pain.

God Is in Control

Do you believe that God is in control? Why or why not? The Bible usually uses the word "sovereign" instead of control, but the meaning is the same. There are plenty of scriptures to support God's sovereignty:

- The Lord has established His throne in heaven; and His kingdom rules over all (Psalm 103:19).
- Our God is in the heaven; He does whatever pleases Him (Psalm 115:3).
- I know that the Lord is great, that our Lord is greater than all gods. The Lord does whatever pleases Him, in the heavens and on the earth, in the seas and all their depths (Psalm 135:5–6).

This includes the animals as well as the weather. With the animals, we read in Exodus 8–10, how God caused frogs, gnats, flies and locusts to invade Egypt. He caused the livestock of Egypt to die. God also caused poisonous snakes to bite people (Numbers 21), hornets to invade (Joshua 24), bears to maul youths (2 Kings 2), and a donkey to rebuke and to talk to Balaam (Numbers 22). In regards to the weather, God caused the world to flood (there is SO much scientific evidence of this) (Genesis 7), a fire to come from heaven upon cities (Genesis 19), the wind to divide the red sea (Exodus 14), the sun to stand still (Joshua 10), a whirlwind to carry Elijah to heaven (2 Kings 2), the rain in answer to Samuel's prayer (1 Samuel 12), a storm to confuse the Philistine army (1 Samuel 7), and darkness during the crucifixion (Matthew 27).

God is also in control over the government (Daniel 4:17), our nation and our workplace (Romans 13:1). He's in control over the stock market, the IRS, and the economy (Luke 16:10, 1 Tim 6:10). He's even in control over you, if you allow Him to be. Are you beginning to see that God is indeed control over everything?

So once we understand that God is indeed in control of all things, we then wonder, "If God is in control, why does He allow bad things to happen?" This is a fair question. But to answer that question, we first need to ask, where does suffering and sin come from? In his book, *The Character of God*, Pastor Billy Crone writes, "Isaiah 14:12-15, the passage describes when the Devil came into existence and his 'fall'. This is where the existence of evil and suffering in the world began. So, suffering began with the devil, not God. Lucifer was at first an angel who, from his overwhelming pride, wanted to be like God, which was never his intended purpose."[2] Which sin does God hate the most? You guessed it, pride. Proverbs 16:5 states, "The LORD detests all the proud of heart. Be sure of this: They will not go unpunished." So God cast Lucifer (now called the devil) down to hell and roam the earth. Once Lucifer fell, it was his mission to turn mankind against God so that we could be infected by the same disease of pride and sin. Once Adam and Eve sinned, this sin, and now the curse of death, was passed down throughout the human race. No one can now live a life without sin or death.

So, what did God do about evil and suffering once it entered our world?

1. God judges evil. (In 1 John 3:8 and in Colossians 2:9–10, 15, states that Jesus Christ stripped the devil of his power).
2. God has put a limit on evil (Job 1:6,9–12).
3. God has made a way out of evil (John 3:16).

As Christians, we should recognize that nothing happens by accident, and that includes our suffering. Everything that happens is within God's plan. Remember that even the apostles suffered greatly, and they were the guys who carried Christ's message to the world! Look over this list written by Pastor Billy Crone and discover just how much the apostles suffered!

1. James, brother of John, was beheaded.
2. Thomas was run through his body with a spear.
3. Simon, brother of Jude, was crucified in Egypt.
4. Simon, the Zealot was crucified.
5. Mark was burned and buried after being dragged through the streets.
6. Bartholomew was beaten, skinned alive, crucified, then beheaded.
7. Andrew was crucified.
8. Matthew was killed by a spear.
9. Philip was stoned and crucified.
10. James was thrown off the temple and then stoned to death.
11. Peter was crucified upside down.
12. Paul was beheaded.
13. Luke was hanged upon an olive tree.
14. Jude was shot to death by arrows.

15. Matthias was first stoned and then beheaded.
16. Barnabas was stoned to death.
17. John was put in a cauldron of boiling oil but survived and later died a 'natural' death.

Pastor Billy Crone states 4 reasons why suffering occurs:

1. Our own sin
2. Other People's Sin
3. Spiritual Warfare
4. For the Glory of God

Pastor Crone then goes on to list 20 possible reasons why God allows difficulties to occur:

(I would highly recommend reading his entire book to explore in detail each of these areas)

1. To Expose our sin nature
2. To keep us from becoming spiritually lazy
3. To cause us to be a blessing to others
4. To learn that God is God and we are not
5. To make us more like Jesus
6. To keep us from wasting our lives
7. To make us more humble
8. To make us more joyful
9. To make us more loving
10. To produce a powerful testimony
11. To produce a powerful character
12. To get you steered into a new direction
13. To get you to appreciate fellowship
14. To get you to build your faith
15. To get you to return to Him
16. To get you to witness for Him
17. To teach you the power of praise
18. To purify your service

19. To discipline you
20. To take you to heaven

As you see, the reasons on this list are ultimately for our good. As Rick Warren always says, "God is much more interested in building your character, than in your comfort." Sometimes we don't think we need God to build our character or for Him to work on us through our suffering. While the suffering lasts, we usually are focused on our pain and are unable to see anything else. But, after a tragedy or heartbreak we occasionally see God's plan immediately. Sometimes we see this plan after some time has passed. And in some instances, we never will see God's plan this side of heaven (Heb. 11:13). If you are in a time of suffering, let me tell you how sorry I am for you, and that I wish you didn't have to go through this experience. My prayer is that you will seek God to carry you through this time and that you lean on His guidance.

I think one of the most difficult lessons to learn in life is that we are not in control. No matter how much we try to be, we just aren't. We need to always be reminded who is, and then relinquish our control to His.

God Is Good

Did you know that the English word "God" is derived from the word "good"?

"GOD - The English word God is identical with the Anglo-Saxon word for 'good,' and therefore it is believed that the name God refers to the divine goodness."[3]

So, when you hear the name of God, you should think of the word good as well. The two words go together.

When my husband was a pastor, he would always say, "God is good!" and then the congregation would reply "All the time!" We loved saying the phrase because we knew in our hearts it was true. After our church merged with another, the other pastor didn't want Kevin to use this saying in church any more. He believed that the phrase "God is good" was too difficult for some people to understand or to believe. Do you believe that God is good? Do you believe that God is good all the time? Why or why not? Decide for yourself after reading the following quote from Bible.org:

From the series: The Joy of Knowing God

"You are good and do only good; teach me your decrees" (Psalm 119:68 NLT). First of all, God Himself is good; that is, He is everything that God should be—the ideal person, the sum total of all perfection. There are no defects or contradictions in Him, and nothing can be added to His nature to make Him any better. He is excellence to an infinite degree, possessing every desirable quality, and therefore of inestimable value. God is good.

Because God is Himself the highest and greatest good, He is also the source and fountain of all other good. He does good things. He extends His goodness to others. It is His nature to be kind, generous, and benevolent, to demonstrate good will toward men, and to take great pleasure in making them happy. Because God is good, He wants us to have what we need for our happiness and He sees that it is available to us. Every good thing we now enjoy or ever hope to enjoy flows from Him, and no good thing has ever existed or ever will exist that does not come from His good hand.

That is why Jesus could say to the rich young ruler, "No one is good except God alone." No other being is infinitely and innately and immutably good. All goodness that exists outside of Him finds its source in Him. Even a man as godly as the Apostle Paul had to admit that in his natural being there was no good thing (Romans 7:18), and we have to admit it too. If there is any good to be found in us, it had to come from God, for we are incapable of producing it ourselves.

In addition, everything God does is good—specially tailored for our benefit. Asaph began Psalm 73 by stating quite literally, "Only God is good to Israel." In other words, God is nothing but good. He can do nothing but what is absolutely best."[4]

So, have you decided if God is truly good or not? I believe that when we come to have enough faith to believe that God is good all the time, it allows us to begin to see the big picture of the events in our lives, both good and bad. Romans 8:28 says, "And we know that in all things God works for the good of those who love Him." This is essentially what we are believing when we put our faith in God's goodness. It allows us to put our entire trust and faith in Him regardless of our circumstances.

God Is Creative

God's creativity is my favorite attribute of God. Being someone who is creative, I love knowing that my creativity comes from God. Rick Warren likes to remind us that, "You are most like God when you are creative." God created everything. The sun, moon, stars, sunsets, oceans, trees, flowers, plants, animals, rainbows, clouds, etc. Everything from nature is from Him and has been designed by Him.

Years ago I would drive in early to my job on an elevated highway which allowed me to see the beautiful sun rise each morning. I would begin to imagine what God's mood was for the day, based on the sun rise I saw that morning. They were breathtaking. Each day the sky displayed colors and shapes different from the days before. God was showing off His creativity.

I see His design and imagination in all that is around me… especially with animals. We currently own nine animals (four chickens, a dog, two cats, a lizard and a turtle) and just love having them around. I can also see that God certainly has a sense of humor when watching my chickens. They are just too funny. We have an instigator chicken and three follower chickens that are always heading into mischief!

But more than that, I am just in awe of God's creativity. Simply by examining the animal kingdom alone, we see the vast differences and beauty in giraffes, elephants, sloths, humming birds, whales, dolphins, ant eaters, dinosaurs, monkeys, pandas, polar bears, horses, llamas, cows, goats (this list could go on forever), each designed specifically by God for a specific purpose. These creatures were designed and created by God and were not formed by accident. In Genesis 1:24–25 the Bible states, "And God said, 'Let the land produce living creatures according to their kinds: livestock, creatures that move along the ground, and wild animals, each according to its kind.' And it was so. God made the wild animals according to their kinds, the livestock according to their kinds, and all the creatures that move along the ground according to their kinds. And God saw that it was good."

God Is Wise

Wisdom should not be mistaken for knowledge, since wisdom goes far and above knowing facts or ideas. It is knowledge, combined with the ability to know precisely how to use that knowledge at the right time, in the right way, and with the right motive.

We all know information that would make us knowledgeable on a certain topic, but is that knowledge the real truth concerning how we should live? With access to a wealth of information just a click away on the internet, it is easy for us to believe we are smart. We enjoy showing off how smart we are by citing sports statistics, quoting movie lines, or by solving a problem at work. But again, that is knowledge, not wisdom.

I think it's been even more difficult to see the wisdom of God today because, in our true nature, we desire and think more highly of other people in our world who have attained knowledge. We go to them for advice. We read their books. We watch their documentaries. But we are not seeking the true wisdom of God. However, when we don't seek God's wisdom, we get into trouble.

One of the individuals who was highly esteemed for his knowledge in his day was Sigmund Freud. His theory was that people should go to a professional psychologist to receive psychoanalysis for help, instead of their pastors. He thought that behavioral and psychological help would come from science, not God. His ideas ended up becoming a detriment to society.

During the 20th century a certain Sigmund Freud had several books published which made a major impact on the world. These books included *The Interpretation of Dreams* (1900), *The Psychopathology of Everyday* Life (1901), and the *Introductory Lectures on Psycho-Analysis* (1915–1916).

Freud set out to show that the experiences, actions and thoughts of everyday life were determined not by our conscious rationality, but by irrational forces completely outside of our conscious life. Freud believed that these forces could only be properly understood and controlled (where necessary) by an extensive treatment process which he called *psychoanalysis*.

Freud was adamantly opposed to Christianity. He taught that religious doctrines are all illusions and that religion is *"A universal obsessional neurosis of humanity."*

In fact, along with sexual repression, he viewed religion as one of the main reasons for mental problems and thus formed all of his notions from a Darwinist, godless position. Yet Freud's views have influenced our culture to the degree that even many Christians began to doubt the effectiveness of the Bible and the Church in dealing with life's problems. All the while, Freud never deviated from his view that belief in God was not only delusionary but actually psychologically damaging. He negatively influenced the faith and affected the attitudes of many people concerning the role of the Church in healing troubled souls. Indeed, he thought it entirely preposterous that people with problems of the mind would be more likely to consult with a Christian minister rather than consult the conclusions of his psychoanalysis. There is strong evidence that he began to see that he could best further his intrinsic Darwinist motivations by *replacing* the position of a rabbi or Christian minister in European society with his scheme of psychoanalysis.

...He claimed that he had developed a *science* of the mind to *replace religion.* The irony of this, however, is that it is now increasingly being accepted that his theories are not—and never were—science of any real kind, and his commitment to them was really a religious kind of acceptance! He imposed his theories upon people who, perhaps somewhat naively, accepted them as a "new science" but society is now facing the truth of the abject failure of Freud and of his psychoanalysis.[5]

Did you know that Freud was also a believer in the positive health benefits of cocaine and was a user himself for many years? He also refused to be psychoanalyzed himself, even by his own teachings. It's difficult to believe that our society has been led astray by this man and his theories. This is another example of how our society for many years, had "exchanged the truth of God for a lie."

In 1 Kings 2:2–4 when King David sent for his son Solomon before he died, he gave him this advice:

"I am about to go the way of all the earth," he said. "So be strong, show yourself a man, and observe what the LORD your God requires: Walk in His ways and keep His decrees and commands, His laws and requirements, as written in the Law of Moses, so that you may prosper in all you do and wherever you go, and that the LORD may keep His promise to me: 'If your descendants watch how they live, and if they walk faithfully before me with all their heart and soul, you will never fail to have a man on the throne of Israel.'"

In order for us to "Walk in His ways, and keep His decrees and commands, His laws and requirements... so that you may prosper in all you do and wherever you go," we need to seek God's wisdom and truth. Shouldn't that be our ultimate goal in life—that we succeed in everything we do so that God's promises concerning us will be fulfilled?

Solomon did take his father David's advice. He asked the Lord for wisdom, which God granted. He became known as the wisest man on earth. Many came to seek his advice throughout the world.

Scriptures that reference God's infinite wisdom:

- Psalm 147:5 "Great is our Lord and mighty in power. His understanding has no limit."
- Romans 11:33 "Oh, the depth of the riches both of the wisdom and knowledge of God! How unsearchable are His judgments and unfathomable His ways!" (NAS)
- Isaiah 55:9 "As the heavens are higher than the earth, so are My ways higher than your ways and My thoughts than your thoughts."

- Jeremiah 10:12 "But God made the earth by His power; He founded the world by His wisdom; and stretched out the heavens by His understanding."
- Psalm 104:24 "How many are Your works, O Lord! In wisdom you made them all; the earth is full of Your creatures."
- Proverbs 3:19–20 "By wisdom the Lord laid the earth's foundations, by understanding He set the heavens in place; by His knowledge the deeps were divided, and the clouds let drop the dew."
- Isaiah 40:12—14 "Who has measured the waters in the hollow of His hand, or with the breadth of His hand marked off the heavens? Who has held the dust of the earth in a basket, or weighed the mountains on the scales and the hills in a balance? Who has understood the mind of the Lord, or instructed Him as his counselor? Whom did the Lord consult to enlighten Him, and who taught Him the right way? Who was it that taught Him knowledge or showed Him the path of understanding?"

God in His infinite wisdom created everything. Just try to wrap your mind around what kind of incredibly powerful wisdom it would take to create the earth, seas, clouds, plants, insects, animals, people, stars and the sun. Sometimes it's hard for us to create our own sandwich, let alone create anything like God has created! Man has tried but has been, for the most part, unsuccessful. This is because life only comes from life. We can't create something from nothing, but God has.

God's wisdom not only is seen in His creation, but also in His counsel. Daniel 2:20–22 states, "Praise be to the name of God for ever and ever; wisdom and power are His. He changes times and seasons; He sets up kings and disposes them. He gives wisdom to the wise and knowledge to the discerning. He reveals deep and hidden things; He knows what lies in darkness, and light dwells with Him." So, if you want direction for your life, it is best to ask the only One who knows our past, our present conditions and our future to guide our lives. I've told students before that when we go through life, it's kind of like going through a maze, where we can't see what's around the next turn. But God sees us within that maze from up above, where He knows the best path for our future.

J. I. Packer has defined wisdom as:

"Wisdom is the power to see, and the inclination to choose, the best and highest goal, together with the surest means of attaining it. Wisdom is, in fact, the practical side of moral goodness. As such, it is found in its fullness only in God. He alone is naturally and entirely and invariably wise."

God is Holy

The concept of the holiness can sometimes be a difficult subject to tackle. Most often it is defined within the Christian culture as "set apart," and is often referred to the way Christians should live. I know that there are many Bible verses that state that we should pursue holiness and live as though we are set apart from the world. However, even though I do agree we should live as though we are set apart, I prefer to concentrate on God, Jesus or the Holy Spirit when I think of a definition of the word "Holy." God's holiness is not just a single attribute of God, but a way to describe all of God's characteristics. For example, God is not just wise, but He has holy wisdom. God displays His holiness by showing us holy truth, holy love and holy justice. God's holiness is so integrated within God, that everything He does is holy. Holy is the only attribute that describes God not one, twice, but three times in Revelation 4:8 (and in Isaiah 6:1–3): "Each of the four living creatures had and was with eyes all around, even under his wings. Day and night they never stop saying: 'Holy, holy, holy is the Lord God Almighty, who was, and is, and is to come.'" In both John's and Isaiah's visions, these beings are continually declaring God's glory. They are declaring that God is so "set apart" that He is separate from sin, corruption, and impurity. He is perfect in all ways; He is extraordinary, in a category all to Himself, unmatched by any other being or thing in the universe. One of the best books written on this subject is a book called *The Holiness of God* by R.C. Sproul, in which he states:

> It's dangerous to assume that because a person is drawn to holiness in his study that he is thereby a holy man. There is irony here. I am sure that the reason I have a deep hunger to learn of the holiness of God is precisely because I am not holy. I am a profane man—a man who spends more time out of the temple than in it. But I have had just enough of a taste of the majesty of God to want more. I know what it means to be a forgiven man and what it means to be sent on a mission. My soul cries for more. My soul needs more.

> The idea of holiness is so central to biblical teaching that it is said of God, "Holy is His name." (Luke 1:49b). His name is holy because He is holy. He is not always treated with holy reverence. His name is tramped through the dirt of this world. It functions as a curse word, a platform for the obscene. That the world has little respect for God is vividly

seen by the way the world regards His name. No honor. No reverence. No awe before Him.

Because God is holy, we should always honor Him and give Him our highest respect. In fact, it's been said, "Irreverence is a dangerous malady." So, in other words, we become dangerously ill (get a disorder, get infected, or become tainted) when we are no longer honoring or have respect for God. I find it ironic that the same word used to describe mental illness today (a disorder), is the same word that is used here to describe what happens to us when we are no longer showing God respect.

The easiest and most exhilarating way for me to give God honor is by worshiping and praising Him through music. After five years of struggling with infertility and then finally conceiving, whenever I would rock our kids to sleep, I would sing praises to God. I was just so incredibly thankful to Him for giving them to me. That was the best way I knew how to show God how much I loved Him for blessing us with our children and for always supplying all our needs.

Not only can we worship God in church by singing to Him, but we can worship Him in all that we do or wherever we are. Our work can be done in such a way that it brings glory to God. We can uplift those around us, by showing God's love to others. We can sing praises to God in the car, or in the shower. Find a way to worship God that works best for you. I promise that whatever bad mood you are in at the time, your spirit will be lifted.

God Is Righteous

Synonyms for the word Righteous are: Virtuous, good, innocent, deserving, praiseworthy, excellent, pure, noble, and just. Righteous means that God's actions are always right and fair. The original Hebrew word from which we get righteousness can also be translated as just or justice. That means that God has no favorites. Unlike us humans, God does not judge based on outer appearance, our past, or what we may think is right or wrong. He will judge us all as we have rightly deserved, according to His standards alone. This is a good thing. His laws are universal and are truly right. No matter where you are from, or what you have learned, or what you believe, everyone knows inherently that there is a right from wrong. For example, we all understand to some degree that murder, lying, adultery, and stealing is wrong. But with other sins, you don't have to guess what is right from wrong when you read His word. It tells you. There are some issues that may be a little vague, but as a whole, God's word is our standard for striving to live righteously.

1. The Lord is righteous in all His ways and loving toward all He has made. (Psalm 145:17)
2. Clouds and thick darkness surround Him; righteousness and justice are the foundation of His throne (Psalm 97:2)

There are many scriptures that reference how we can become righteous in God's eyes, which can only come through Christ and by what He has done for us.

1. By making peace (James 3:18)
2. By believing in the Lord (Genesis 15:6) (Romans 10:4)
3. By practicing and pursuing righteousness (1John 2:29) (2 Tim. 2:22)
4. By hungering and thirsting for righteousness (Matthew 5:6)

5. By having and living by faith (Romans 4:5) (Romans 1:17)
6. By confessing our sins (1 John 1:9)
7. By observing justice and knowing the rights of the poor (Psalm 106:3) (Proverbs 29:7)
8. By praying for others (James 5:16)
9. By repenting and being remorseful over our sin, and then by fleeing from temptation (Daniel 9:24)
10. By allowing God to test us (Psalm 11:5)
11. By allowing Scripture to train us (2 Tim. 3:16)
12. By submitting to God's righteousness (Romans 10:3)
13. By fearing God (Malachi 4:2)
14. By doing what is just and right (Ezekiel 18:5–9)
15. Is not a result of works (Titus 3:5)

God is Near

Psalm 139:1–12, written by King David, in my opinion, describes God's nearness well:

> O Lord, you have searched me, and you know me. You know when I sit and when I rise; you perceive my thoughts from afar. You discern my going out and lying down; you are familiar with all my ways. Before a word is on my tongue you know it completely, O Lord. You hem me in—behind and before; you have laid your hand upon me. Such knowledge is too wonderful for me, too lofty for me to attain. Where can I go from your Spirit? Where can I flee from your presence? If I go up to the heavens, you are there; if I make my bed in the depths, you are there. If I rise on the wings of the dawn, if I settle on the far sides of the sea, even there your hand will guide me, your right hand will hold me fast. If I say, "Surely the darkness will hide me and the light become night around me," even the darkness will not be dark to you; the night will

shine like the day, for darkness is as light to you. (Psalm 139: 1–12)

So according to King David, God is always near us. There is nowhere we can escape from God, no matter how much we try to hide from Him. He knows our thoughts, motives, actions, feelings and secrets. He knows what we're going to do, and why we're going to do it. He knows us better than we know ourselves. Sometimes this can make us afraid of God, thinking that if God really knew us, He wouldn't like us or scold us somehow. But be assured, God is not like that. He loves us and wants to encourage us. God loves us so much that He gave His only Son to die for us. In fact, Immanuel (another name for Jesus) means "God with us."

Psalm 73:23–26 describes how the ultimate blessing in life is not success, prosperity, or the absence of pain, but the presence of God which states, "Yet I am always with you; you hold me by my right hand. You guide me with your counsel, and afterward you will take me into glory. Whom have I in heaven but you? And earth has nothing I desire besides you. My flesh and my heart may fail, but God is the strength of my heart and my portion forever." Do you sense that God is close to you? Why or why not? What can you do to feel closer to God?

God Is Joyful

Do you believe God is joyful? I think sometimes we get the impression that God is always in a bad mood, just waiting to judge and punish us. Perhaps this comes from having judgmental parents, teachers, or other authority figures in our lives that have treated us this way. But let me assure you, God is not like that. God is sorrowful when we sin, but God is also loving, patient and kind, as well as joyful. The word joy is defined as "happy, delight, gladness, sunshine, cheerfulness, elation." God found joy (or was delighted) in His creation. Several times in Genesis is the phrase "and God saw that it was good." Moses indicated God's joy of His creation by repeating to us that God saw that His creation was good, just like when we experience joy when we create something we are proud of.

When we are happy, or joyful, we smile. God does too. Numbers 6:24–26 (NLT) says, "May the Lord bless you and protect you. May the Lord **smile** on you and be gracious to you. May the Lord show you His favor and give you His peace." But joy isn't just God's character, but He also gives us joy. Jesus told His disciples they would have great joy in John 15:11, which states, "I have told you this so that my joy may be in you and that your joy may be complete." And in John 17:13, He states, "But now I have come to Thee; and these things I speak in the world, that they may have My joy made full in themselves." One of my favorite verses is 1 Thes. 5:16–18, which states, "Be joyful always; pray continually, give thanks in all circumstances; for this is God's will for you in Christ Jesus." Perhaps if we prayed continually, and gave thanks in all circumstances, we would rejoice always!

True joy is the result of being restored by God, because of what God has done for us. It's when we become who God has intended us to be. It's when our hearts are whole and we become healed. I lived for many years being unhappy because of the pain within me. Now that I've experienced God's healing, I am truly happy, content, and have peace (most of the time). I still have more within me to become healed, but God has done some amazing work within my heart. He has taken what was once broken and has gently restored me to become more of who God has created me to be. My hope is that you will experience the same inner joy.

One of the outcomes of inner joy is laughter. I have gone to churches where people within the congregation are most often unhappy. I'm not saying that we should fake happiness if we aren't. But I am strongly suggesting that if you are unhappy, that you'll begin to ask God why and allow Him to heal you. A good indication of a healthy church is if you hear laughter often. I think that is my favorite part about our church. Any time I walk through the halls, I hear laughter. I think God loves hearing laughter too.

Does God have a sense of humor? If we remember that we are created in God's image, then it stands to reason that our sense of humor comes from God. I think God loves humor. I think, just like us, He loves to smile and laugh. But there is a difference between the humor found in our fallen world, which can be crude and evil, versus the humor of God, which is pure and wholesome. For instance, who can look at a llama's face, with

its' bucked teeth, or a long-nosed monkey, or an ostrich and not see God's sense of humor?

God Is Forgiving

God forgives us for our sins. In 1 John 1:9 the Bible states, "If we confess our sins, He is faithful and just and will forgive us our sins and to purify us from all unrighteousness." But first, we need to acknowledge that we have sinned, and that we have been disobedient to God. All of us sin. 1 John 1:8 states, "If we claim to be without sin, we deceive ourselves, and the truth is not in us." The amazing thing is that God is always ready to forgive us completely, no matter what we've done. No sin is unforgiveable.

But we often times forget that our forgiveness is directly tied to how easily we can forgive others. Matthew 6:14–15 states, "For if you forgive men when they sin against you, your heavenly Father will also forgive you. But if you do not forgive men their sins, your father will not forgive your sins." To be honest with you, this verse scares me. I personally have a difficult time forgiving others. But for God to forgive me, I know I must (not should) forgive those around me who have hurt me. Sometimes we like to wallow in the pain caused by others. But we need to understand that by not forgiving, we are just making ourselves miserable. The act of forgiveness is not letting someone off the hook for what they have done, but for us to rely on God and for Him to heal us from our pain. We should want to forgive others because God has forgiven us. Forgiveness can be immediate, but trust can be lost and needs to be rebuilt. I have found that forgiveness is much easier when God has shown me the reason I got hurt or offended in the first place; usually by revealing a lie that I have believed. Once God shows me the truth to replace that lie, then my feelings tend to follow and I am able to forgive much more easily.

Since many families do not model forgiveness well, it doesn't come easy or natural to us. Forgiveness is a process that must be learned. The more often we forgive, the easier it becomes. But I also think there are many times when someone either asks us to forgive them right away, or when we may want to forgive someone right away, but when time is really needed to process forgiveness completely and for bitterness not to return. How often have we thought we have forgiven someone, just for the bitterness to return unexpectedly, almost as strong, or stronger, than it was before? It can catch us by surprise, often from some trigger of a memory or feeling. If you are having difficulty in forgiving someone, ask God why. Ask Him to show you the truth behind the lie that you have believed. Give your pain over to God to heal you and quit carrying the bitterness that is eating you up inside.

I think the world would be such a better place if we just learned to say "I'm sorry." Too often, these words are never said. I've heard people say, "Well, that's water under the bridge." Or, "You can't cry over spilt milk." These are words people say when they should have said "I'm sorry." I don't know why those two words are so difficult for so many people to say, but they are. It takes humility and great strength to admit you are sorry, but nothing reconnects a relationship quite like it. Those words are not only incredibly powerful, but amazingly healing. However, even if we never receive an "I'm sorry," we are still called to forgive.

God's Wrath

Of all of the characteristics of God, I think the trait that we most fear is God's wrath. We'd rather think about God's love for us and His mercy. However, there are more scripture verses about the anger, fury and wrath of God, than there are of His love and kindness. We need to remember, however, that God's divine wrath is different that the wrath we may experience from those around us. Unlike human wrath, which is usually generated by sin within that person, God's wrath is always provoked by sins committed by the human race. It is a righteous anger. In fact, God brings glory to Himself when He expresses His wrath. He'll fight for the righteous. He'll protect the innocent. He'll judge those who sin against others. However, we also need to keep in mind that He'll punish us we when don't obey Him. I think sometimes we really underestimate just how much God hates sin. His wrath is always in direct proportion to our sin, so when we experience His wrath, it is our fault. God's wrath should motivate us to live a life as pure as possible, and to repent when we mess up. Just like our loving parents disciplined us to keep us from harming ourselves or others, we can be disciplined by God as well. It is for our own good, and is supposed to make us desire to restore our relationship with God.

The person who most experienced God's wrath was Jesus. He took on the full punishment for our sin and became our "scapegoat" for the wrath that we rightly deserved. Even though God loved His Son dearly, Jesus became the object of God's wrath. Jesus satisfied God's holy wrath by laying our sins on Himself and taking on the full punishment for them. When we don't confess our sins and allow Jesus to take those sins to the cross for us, we may also experience God's wrath, especially when we die. If we don't confess our sins and believe that Jesus died for us and rose again, we will experience eternal judgement, which is hell. Let me assure you that hell is a frightening place. It is a place of weeping and gnashing of teeth (Luke 13:28, Matthew 13:42). It is a place of torment and sorrow. It is a place of no rest, hopelessness and suffering. If you don't know if you'll be going to heaven or not, and would like to begin a relationship with God, I would urge you to pray this (or similar to) this prayer:

> *Lord Jesus, I ask You to forgive my sins and save me from eternal separation from God. By faith, I accept Your work and death on the cross as sufficient payment for my sins. Thank You for providing the way for me to know You and to have a relationship with my heavenly Father. Through faith in You, I have eternal life. Thank You also for hearing my prayers and loving me unconditionally. Please give me the strength, wisdom, and determination to walk in the center of Your will. In Jesus' name, amen.* [6]

God's Grace

Have you ever thought that you were too sinful to be forgiven? That you were too far gone to be accepted by God? My husband Kevin had a friend who once said, "If I would go to church, then the walls would fall down." This man committed a crime that he thought was unforgiveable. Many years before, he had come home and found his wife in bed with another man. He was so hurt and so angry that he then took this man's life. Even though he had served for years in jail for his crime, he still felt sinful and had no hope of ever being restored. Unfortunately, a couple of years later, this man committed suicide. He just couldn't accept that God would forgive him, that God loved him and that God would show him grace. You see, just like Kevin's friend, at the deepest core of ourselves, we are all underserving of God's grace. But He gives it anyway. And He gives it freely and abundantly.

I think of all of God's characteristics, His grace should be the most prized. "Grace" is unmerited or undeserved favor of God. In His grace, God is willing to forgive us and bless us abundantly, in spite of the fact that we have sinned and don't deserve to be treated generously or even fairly. It's is God's most precious gift to us. Jesus came to save us all. He loved to be with those who were humble and knew that they were not perfect and needed a savior. He loved hanging out with those who were considered the lowest class of that society. Every sinner is lost and doomed to be damned, apart from the grace of God. Paul had once described himself as the "chief of sinners" (1 Timothy 1:15). He had persecuted and was responsible for killing Christians for years before he himself became a Christian. If God has shown Paul grace, He will certainly show us grace if we allow

Him to. We also need to remember that we are saved by God's grace, and not by our works. No matter how much we do for God's kingdom or how little we do, it has no bearing on God's grace to us. It is totally undeserved. That's what makes it so awesome!

God's Truth

Did you know that Jesus said seventy times in the Gospels of Mathew, Mark, Luke and John, "I tell you the truth..." (1984 NIV)? Why would He say that? Some people have questioned, "Well if those are the only times Jesus said the truth, then has He been saying lies the rest of the time"? The answer is a 100% definite NO! The original Greek text uses the word "amen," which has been translated today as "the truth." Today we have lost the original meaning of this word, by usually just uttering the word "amen" when we have ritualistically ended our prayer or when we have ended a praise song. But the word has several meanings. When "amen" is at the beginning of a sentence, it means "truth," valid, sure, or binding and is centered on the idea of the truth of God. When it is at the end of a sentence, or after a song or prayer, it means "so it is" or "may it be fulfilled." So, when you are saying "amen" at the end of a prayer or a song, you are essentially saying "I believe this is or will come true" (NAS New Testament Greek Lexicon).

But when Jesus repeatedly states seventy-eight times in the gospels, "I tell you the truth" (and repeats this twice each time in the gospel of John), He is not only saying that His words are absolutely true. He is emphasizing that His words are true BE-CAUSE HE IS TRUTH. Jesus and His words are not just true, but truth itself. Every word that Jesus ever spoke was true and important. By repeating "Truly, truly, …" He is stating that we should pay extra close attention to what He is about to say, because it is of the most utmost importance and urgency. Our response should also be urgent and in full submission to it.

In John 14:6, Jesus states "I am the way and the Truth and the life, no one comes to the Father, except through me." In the Jewish Bible, The Message, The Millennium Bible, the Weymouth New Testament, and in the King James Version 21st Century (as well as in another five different bible versions), the word "truth" is capitalized, because it is referring to a person, The Truth, who is Jesus personified. Telling us the truth is His whole purpose. Since Jesus is Truth, He simply cannot lie. When Pontius Pilate asked Jesus what He had done that provoked his own people and chief priests to turn Him in, Jesus replied, "... I have been born and have come into the world for this reason—to testify the truth. Everyone who belongs to the truth listens to my voice." Pilate then asked, "What is truth?" (John 18:37–38). What Pilot didn't realize is that The Truth was standing right in front of him.

Many people don't know what truth is anymore because they don't know how to recognize it. Our society, and especially our colleges today, want to teach "relative truth" instead of "The Truth." Opinions are relative and can change, but the truth will always be the truth. We are constantly bombarded by so-called "facts," which are really just opinions. These opinions, which are masked as "facts" that are coming from the news, textbooks,

TV and the internet are just not true. Instead they are opinions made by biased people in an attempt to win us over to their way of thinking.

John 8:31–32 reads "To the Jews who had believed Him, Jesus said, 'If you hold to my teaching, you are really my disciples. Then you will know the truth, and the truth will set you free'" (John 8:31–32). Jesus is actually saying "If you get to know Me personally and do what I have said for you to do (both in scripture and what He has told us personally), since I am the Truth, you will know the truth, and that truth will set you free" (my interpretation). So if what you hear aligns with scripture and to what you believe Jesus is telling you, then it is true. If it doesn't, then it's false. It's that simple. Of course there are exceptions to this that include those things that are not in scripture, but if you ask God to tell you what the truth is (about any subject or any circumstance), then He should reveal that truth to you **(please read Chapter 8 on prayer first so that you will learn the steps to test what you've heard is actually from God or not!).** But keep in mind that sometimes this truth is revealed over time.

But not only will knowing what is true inform us, it will transform us. Knowing the truth about ourselves, opens our eyes to where we need to grow. It humbles us, and helps us to become reliant on Him in order for us to change. Knowing what is true about those around us will help us become more compassionate and kind to others. It'll help us see others as God sees them, and not how the world would typically see them. Knowing what is true about our society will give us a burden and a desire to help in those areas where God has called us. Hearing God's truth will also heal us. I'll be spending more time on this subject in Chapters 7–10.

God's Glory

There are different things that come to mind when I think of God's glory. In the Old Testament, the original Hebrew word for glory refers to the idea of heaviness and weight. In the New Testament, the word glory carries the idea of opinion, judgment, splendor and brightness. It is used to speak of great honor, praise, value, wonder and splendor. The word glory appears a total of 285 in the Bible, of which the phrase "Glory of the Lord" appears 77 times.

I love the word glory to describe God. It wraps up all that God is. The word Glory incorporates all of His characteristics into one: His splendor, His majesty, His Love, His mercy, and His wrath against sin. It also refers to His radiant light. When I picture God, I picture Himself surrounded in bright light. The Apostle John said that "God is light" in 1 John 1:5. In Revelation, John predicted that God would illuminate the New Jerusalem so brightly that it would have no need for the sun or moon. Whenever God is present with a human, His light is so bright and powerful that no one can look into it. It is only His light that can remove the darkness of pride, sin, and pain in this world.

God's glory is so wonderful, so powerful, and so majestic, that it demands a response from us. Our goal in life should be to glorify God and to honor Him in all that we do. Instead of seeking recognition for ourselves, we should make God's glory known to those around us. We should tell others about what He has done for us, praise Him, and seek His wisdom in every step that we take and then give Him the credit for everything that is good in our lives. "So whether you eat or drink or whatever you do, do it all to the glory of God" (1 Corinthians 10:31).

Good job! You hung in there! Doesn't knowing and understand God's character traits really help with knowing just how awesome He is and how much we can trust Him with our most precious thoughts, hurts, fears, grief and sin? The next step is to begin to interrogate our thoughts. After that, the real healing begins.

CHAPTER 6 | Interrogating Our Temptations

(Taking Every Thought Captive)

n order to understand why we are tempted, we need to first understand the root of all sin. Recently I posted a poll on Facebook asking the question:

"What do you think the root cause of sin is?

A. Pride/Selfishness

B. Past emotional pain

C. An altered (incorrect) view of God.

D. The root cause may be different in each case.

E. Another reason _____ (fill in the blank)."

Well, needless to say, I didn't have many responses (although many "liked" my post). Perhaps people haven't really thought about it, or that they just don't know. Most people are taught that we were all born inherently with sin, since the fall of man in the Garden of Eden. We have also been taught that we sin because we want to play God and run our lives in our own way (Answer A). Oswald Chambers, however, pointed out that the root of sin lies in "an incurable suspicion of God": that we don't believe that God is good or that we have an incorrect view of God, which would make that the correct answer (Answer C). I don't think many of us would admit that we don't believe God is good, but when we sin, that is exactly what we are believing at that moment. We think that what we want (anything we are tempted with) is more important that what God wants for us.

I think it is easy for our view of God to become altered because every relationship around us is to some degree dysfunctional. We haven't witnessed first-hand what a perfect relationship is like. So, when we replace God's correct characteristic with our own warped view, we become much more vulnerable to sin.

Genesis Chapter 3: The Fall of Man

Now the serpent was more crafty than any of the wild animals the LORD God had made. He said to the woman, "Did God really say, 'You must not eat from any tree in the garden'?"

The woman said to the serpent, "We may eat fruit from the trees in the garden, but God did say, 'You must not eat fruit from the tree that is in the middle of the garden, and you must not touch it, or you will die.'"

"You will not certainly die," the serpent said to the woman. "For God knows that when you eat from it your eyes will be opened, and you will be like God, knowing good and evil."

When the woman saw that the fruit of the tree was good for food and pleasing to the eye, and also desirable for gaining wisdom, she took some and ate it. She also gave some to her husband, who was with her, and he ate it. Then the eyes of both of them were opened, and they realized they were naked; so they sewed fig leaves together and made coverings for themselves.

Then the man and his wife heard the sound of the LORD God as He was walking in the garden in the cool of the day, and they hid from the LORD God among the trees of the garden. But the LORD God called to the man, "Where are you?"

He answered, "I heard you in the garden, and I was afraid because I was naked; so I hid."

And He said, "Who told you that you were naked? Have you eaten from the tree that I commanded you not to eat from?"

The man said, "The woman you put here with me— she gave me some fruit from the tree, and I ate it."

Then the LORD God said to the woman, "What is this you have done?" (Genesis 3:1–13)

I noticed that there were a few lies stated before the original sin took place. A lie can be defined as a false statement made with deliberate intent to deceive; an intentional untruth; a falsehood:

- Lie #1: Satan insinuated doubt about God: "Can it really be that God has said?" He misrepresented God as forbidding Adam and Eve to eat of every tree.
- Lie #2: Eve said, "You shall not eat from it nor touch it, otherwise you will die." But God had said nothing about *touching* the tree.
- Lie #3: Satan said, "You certainly will not die! For God knows that when you eat from it your eyes will be opened [that is, you will have greater awareness], and you will be like God, knowing [the difference between] good and evil." Satan flatly contradicted God about the inevitability of judgment on those who disobeyed, just as his followers still deny the facts of hell and eternal punishment. Satan misrepresented God as seeking to withhold from Adam and Eve something that would have been beneficial to them.[1]

So, temptation and then the first sin initially stemmed from lies that Satan said about God in order to change our perception of God and mistrust Him. When God asked Eve, "What is this that you have done?" Eve replied, "The serpent beguiled (charmed, or enchanted in a deceptive way or tricked) *and* deceived me, and I ate [from the forbidden tree]."

In studying Genesis, I wondered who was ultimately responsible for the origination of sin. Was it Adam and Eve because they intentionally disobeyed? Was it Satan because he deceived them? Or could both be at fault? However, in Romans 1:18–25 it states the progression of sin:

> The wrath of God is being revealed from heaven against all the godlessness and wickedness of people, who suppress the truth by their wickedness, since what may be known about God is plain to them, because God has made it plain to them. For since the creation of the world God's invisible qualities—his eternal power and divine nature—have been clearly seen, being understood from what has been made, so that people are without excuse. For although they knew God, they neither glorified Him as God nor gave thanks to Him, but their thinking became futile and their foolish hearts were darkened. Although they claimed to be wise, they became fools and exchanged the glory of the immortal God for images made to look like a mortal human being and birds and animals and reptiles. Therefore, God gave them over in the sinful desires of their hearts to sexual impurity for the degrading of their bodies with one another. They exchanged the truth about God for a lie, and worshiped and served created things rather than the Creator—who is forever praised. Amen.

So, since God gave us proof of His existence by just observing the overwhelming evidence of His creation around us, we are without excuse for not believing in God and of His true character. Even though in their hearts people know God exists, some have chosen not to honor, give thanks to, or to worship God. Instead, many have chosen to rely on their own knowledge, which is foolish and have resulted in darkening their hearts. They willfully exchanged the truth of God for a lie and have, perhaps unknowingly, served and worshiped themselves or Satan instead.

That means that sin is intentional, and that even though it begins with a lie or a temptation that was implanted within our minds, which may have come from the devil and was unintentional, it is our responsibility to act or not to act on that sin. But because there is a progression of sin before it is committed, there is a chance to stop it before it becomes a reality if we learn to take every thought captive. That is why interrogating our thoughts is so important. In 2 Corinthians 10:5 it states, "We break down every thought and proud thing that puts itself up against the wisdom of God. We take hold of every thought and make it obey Christ" (NLV).

So, just like we interrogate criminals or prisoners when they are arrested here in the U.S., we should also interrogate our thoughts by taking them captive. When the U.S. government or law enforcement interrogates a suspect they often use a series of questions from the "Reid Technique of Interrogation" in order to guide the suspect into a true confession. However, the questions are different when it comes to interrogating our thoughts (Taken from Pastor Rick Warren's "Can you Hear me Now?" series):

- Question 1: Does this thought align with the Bible? If you are struggling in a certain area, then I would recommend studying (and memorizing) verses that pertain to that temptation. You can do this by looking at a topical concordance sometimes included in the back of Bibles, by using a separate topical concordance, or by searing a certain topic on the internet at a reputable, biblically-based website like BibleGateway.com. This is why memorizing scripture is important—so that you can instantly know if this is a thought that is scripturally based or not. If it isn't, then chances are it's coming from our own desires or from Satan.

- Question 2: Does this thought attack my value as a person? Are you having thoughts like, "I'm stupid," "No one likes me," "I'm ugly," "I'm worthless"… then chances are those thoughts are coming from Satan. It's one thing to have those thoughts every so often, but it's another when we actually start believing those thoughts and they begin to take over our thought life. We will begin to believe them if we don't attack them head on and recognize these thoughts as lies. You can help eradicate those thoughts by studying scripture that talks about how much God loves you, how you were intricately woven and created by Him, and that He has called you for a specific purpose. Remember that God has never had a bad thought about you and never will.

- Question 3: Is this thought convicting or condemning?

Condemnation vs. Conviction

<u>Conviction:</u>

From God
Temporary until you confess

Specific
Purpose is to correct something in your life
God will never attack my personal value

Condemnation:

From Satan
Lasts for days, weeks or even years
General
Purpose is to make you miserable
Satan attacks your personal value
(You're stupid, You're worthless, You're unloved, etc.)

PHASE TWO SUMMARY AND DISCUSSION QUESTIONS

PHASE TWO SUMMARY:

L = Replacing <u>Lies</u> with the Truth
- Why memorizing scripture is important.
- Understanding how much God loves us will help heal us.
- Learning to trust in God's character.
- How to take every thought captive.

DISCUSSION QUESTIONS:

1. Did you see any scriptures that would be good for you to memorize that would help combat any self-defeating thought or lies that you may have?

2. Describe how much you think God loves you. Is this an area that you struggle believing in? Why or why not?

3. Did you make the list of what you originally thought were characteristics of God and then throw it away? How and why do you think that

list (or what thoughts have you had previously about God) differ from the list in this book?

4. Were there any characteristics of God that you have now just learned, or didn't completely understand before?

5. How does knowing the true character traits of God help you be able to come to Him with your pain?

6. Have you ever taken any of your self-defeating thoughts captive before? Why or why not?

PRAYER TIME:

Ask God to show you scriptures that would be good for you to memorize, and to help you understand His depth of love for you.

Ask God to keep showing you His true characteristics so that you can continue to believe in and rely on Him.

PHASE 3: LETTING GO

Overcoming What Is Keeping You from Getting Emotionally Healthy

CHAPTER 7 | CLOWNS, BUGS, AND ZOMBIES

(CONFRONTING OUR FEARS)

C hapman University once did a survey on American fears. In that survey, they discovered that the biggest fear among Americans is public speaking (about 25.3%), with the 2nd biggest fear being the fear of heights (24%). The next largest fears were bugs, snakes and other animals, at 22%, and towards the bottom of the list were clowns, which was at 7.6%, which somewhat surprised me (clowns… really?). But what surprised me most about the survey was that 8.9% of Americans had a fear of zombies. Of the top 12 things Americans are afraid of, zombies ranked 9 out of the top 12.[1] Isn't it a little weird to you that almost 9% of Americans fear zombies, something that doesn't even exist?

Fear of healing is another unnecessary anxiety. Most people want to be healed of their hurts but don't want to go through the actual healing process because they are afraid of re-living the pain from the past, even if it's momentary. Like the fear of zombies or clowns, this is a fear that is unnecessary and hinders us from living the life we were meant to experience. Michael Mangis (a professor at Wheaten college) states (regarding resolving pain), "In fact, it usually takes less energy and time to bring resolution to their pain than the time and energy they invested over the years in avoiding the pain."

For years I didn't want to talk about my parents' divorce, because I knew it would bring up all of the old painful memories and that I would need to re-live the pain that I had been so desperate to avoid. But once I finally did receive healing, I was really frustrated with myself that I hadn't experienced it much earlier in my life. Healing made such a vast difference in my attitudes, my reactions to situations, and in my relationships with others. I don't know what took me so long… I guess we just get used to carrying the pain around with us (like the forty pounds of poo) and sometimes it actually becomes part of our identity.

My husband, Kevin, and I have seen too many people in the church who appeared to have become martyrs making pain a part of their identity. So much so that they just can't move past it. Please don't let that happen to you. Keep in mind that sometimes God will choose to not heal us immediately and the healing process may take time. Michael Mangis states, "To those who pray for immediate healing and an end to their pain, either through supernatural or medical means, God sometimes answers no. In God's perfect plan there are reasons why long-term struggles are often best for the development of our souls. By itself, ending psychological pain is not an adequate goal. The most significant growth in human character typically comes through pain." Mangis also states, "People in pain often know intuitively that they have inner spiritual work to do, and they sense they have the inner strength to make meaning from their pain." Our goal should be to heal little by little throughout the rest of our lives so that we can then grow spiritually where God wants us to grow. We can then use our previously painful experiences to help others.

Instead, many times, we think by sharing and re-sharing and then sharing again what had happened to us, we will receive sympathy from others and that that is what will heal us. It'll relieve some stress, and it may bond us with others a little more, but it won't heal you. Only God can heal you. I have seen many people spend a lot of money over the years going to a counselor, but years later they are still exactly the same. If you are going to a counselor for that amount of time, you should expect change to take place and to feel less and less pain over time. If counseling has not helped you, or if going to your friends hasn't helped you, I simply ask that you begin to put your confidence in the one true healer—God. Begin to open your heart to what God has for you, let go of your fears, and expect a great healing to take place by following these simple steps:

1. To become truly healed, you must be committed to healing. I know that seems obvious, but sometimes it isn't. We often like to wallow in our pain and love the attention it gives us. We often like to wallow in our pain and love the attention if gives us. As a symbol of your commitment, sign the contract below and begin the healing process by submitting your fears, excuses, and control over to God. Place the contract where you can see it each day as a visual reminder of the commitment you are making to God and yourself.

2. Tell others whom can keep you accountable of your intention to be healed.

3. Find an accountability and prayer partner that you can trust who you can confess your sins to on a bi-weekly or monthly basis.

HEALING CONTRACT

I, _____, hereby agree and commit to take the following steps to improve my emotional health to God and to myself:

1. I will continue to memorize scripture that best applies to my incorrect thinking.

2. I will continue learning about God's character, especially where I struggle in my perception of God.

3. I will continue to learn and to believe just how much God loves me on a daily basis.

4. I will continue to take every thought captive and to stay away from temptation.

5. I will submit my fears, my control and my excuses to avoid healing over to God.

6. I will have faith in His power to heal me… in His timing and in His way.

(Your Name)_____(Date)_____

CHAPTER 8 | YOU HAVE NOT BECAUSE YOU ASK NOT

(THE POWER OF PRAYER)

One of the things I've noticed while visiting many churches, is that they tend to fall into one of two categories: Scripture based, or Holy Spirit based. What I mean by that is some churches tend to rely mostly, if not completely, on what the scriptures say for their direction. Other churches tend to rely mostly on what the Holy Spirit may be telling them. What I'd like to propose is something radical to both kinds of churches; that we rely BOTH on scripture as well as the Holy Spirit for individual and corporate direction! Scripture reading and memorizing, as well as listening to the Holy Spirit are equally and vitally important in our Christian walk. The two really go hand-in-hand. Unfortunately, I've seldom seen both operate within a church equally and effectively.

We talked about the importance of reading scripture and scripture memory in a previous chapter, so in this chapter I'll primarily be going over the importance of prayer (listening to the Holy Spirit). Prayer must become a larger part of our lives. A recent study shared that the average person only spends about 3–7 minutes a day in prayer (including meal time prayers). I think if people would realize just how much we could potentially experience in our prayer life, that average time would become much higher. I never realized the full potential of prayer before I began having actual conversations with God. Now I haven't had many of those experiences, but when I have they have been very powerful, emotional, and have changed my life.

I know there are many of you who are out there that are very skeptical of the idea of having conversations with God. I understand that because for many years I was skeptical as well. But the Bible has hundreds of scriptures that refer to God speaking, us listening to His voice, and of God giving direction to His people. In fact, the Bible wouldn't have been written if it weren't for the fact that God spoke to His people and then those faithful followers recorded what He said to them. So, if God spoke to all those that are in the Bible, He can certainly speak to us today. We just need to have an open heart and mind, be quiet before God to hear His voice, and be willing to do whatever He tell us. In Jeremiah 33:3 God says to His people, "Call to me and I will answer you and tell you great and unsearchable things you do not know." Job 33:14–17 states: "For God speaks again and again, though people do not recognize it. He speaks in dreams, in visions of the night, when deep sleep falls on people as they lie in their beds. He whispers in their ears and terrifies them with warnings. He makes them turn from doing wrong; He keeps them from pride" (NLT). Jesus says in John 10:27, "My sheep **listen to my voice**; and I know them, and they follow me" (emphasis mine). Luke 11:28 it says, "Blessed rather are those who **hear** the word of God and obey it" (emphasis mine). These verses refers to **hearing** God's voice which is different than **meditating** on God's word. As I mentioned earlier there are thousands of references to hearing God's voice as opposed to only eighteen verses that speaking about meditating on God's word. (Please, don't misunderstand me. Studying and memorizing scripture is equally as important as prayer!)

When I talk about hearing from God, I'm not referring to an audible voice, but usually an impression that one gets from God. For example, sometimes a scripture may come to mind, when you most likely need it. Other times you may get an impression (a still small voice) or a thought that you know is not your own. Sometimes God will put a person's name and circumstance in your mind that you are meant to pray for. God tends to talk to us most often when we are relaxed and our minds are free. I know this sounds weird, but I most often hear from God while I'm taking a bath! Sometimes I hear from God during the middle of the night in which he'll wake me up, or I might have an impression that's laid on my heart when I wake up the next day. Rick Warren has stated that he often will ask God a question before he goes to bed, and by morning an answer will come to his mind.

Other times I've had conversations with God when I've gone to a place where there are no distractions, poured out my heart to God, asked Him questions and then waited. Sometimes I had to empty my mind of things I had to remember or do by writing them down so that my mind would first be free. Then, I listened. God almost always showed up! He healed me of past hurts, replaced lies that I had believed with the truth, and had comforted me. The times when He didn't respond, I realized I first needed to confess the things I knew that were wrong in my life and in my heart.

God's voice can also become visual when He places an image in your mind. There are plenty of examples of people who have received visions from God (Abraham, Joseph, Jacob, Job,

Isaiah, Daniel, Jonah, Peter, Mary… as well as many others). In Habakkuk 1:1 it says, "This is the message that the prophet Habakkuk received in a **vision**" (NLT) (emphasis mine). God's voice can also become visual when He places an image within your mind, or during a dream. So, as you see, God can speak to you in many ways. We just need to expect Him to.

When I've mentioned to others within the church, especially those churches that are more scripture based, about my conversations with God, they seem to shy away from the topic. I think it is a touchy subject because there are people who abuse this concept of "hearing from God." It is good to be cautious in this area. We need to make sure we are listening to the Holy Spirit instead of our own desires or what Satan may be planting in our minds. People can be led astray to think they are hearing from God when they really aren't, and it can cause them to do and say weird things. Sometimes that vision you think you received during a dream could be the result of some bad pizza you had the night before! However, there are ways to test to make sure that what you've heard is actually from God or not. The following is a list to ask yourself from Rick Warren's "Can you Hear Me Now" series (some of these questions you'll notice we also included in Chapter 6). If any of these seven questions answer "no," then it's safe to say, it's not from God:

1. Does it agree with the Bible? This is the #1-way God speaks to us. If you are never reading the Bible, God isn't speaking to you very much. Everything in scripture is God's word. All of it is useful for teaching, for helping people, for correcting them and showing us how to live. "Your

word is lamp to my feet and a light for my path" (Psalm 119:105).

2. Does this impression make me more like Christ? Does this impression help me to develop more love, joy, peace, kindness, goodness, gentleness, faithfulness and self-control? Does this impression give me a larger burden to help others? Does this impression make me love and want to serve God more? Does this impression help me understand how and where God can use me?

3. Does my church family confirm this idea? Rick Warren has stated that the biggest two reasons why people mess up in life is because either: 1) They do not have any spiritually mature friends, or 2) They don't ask or listen to their spiritually mature friends for advice. (Ephesians 3:10) (Proverbs 11:9) (Proverbs 11:14) Don't just look for the answer you want, but what is the truth.

4. Is it consistent with how God has shaped me? (Spiritual gifts, Heart, Ability, Personality, Experience) Your shape will reveal your purpose. He's made you a certain way for a specific purpose.

5. Does it concern my responsibility? Listen for God to speak to you and to your life, not someone else's (like your spouse). Don't ever use "God told me to tell you..." (This can be manipulating). God may speak to you through others, but they are almost always unaware of it. Or it may be a confirmation to you from God that is already confirmed to them. Sometimes God does tell us something about someone, but let God have an opportunity to let that person hear from Him first (Romans 14). However, there may be times when we need to confront someone in love, but we need to be careful that it does not become outside of our responsibility.

6. Is it convicting, rather than condemning? Once you become a Christian, conviction comes from God, and condemnation comes from the devil (Romans 8:1). A lot of Christians live

under condemnation of the devil, thinking it's from God, but it's not. The purpose of conviction is to correct something that is out-of-whack in your life. The purpose of condemnation is just to put you down and make you feel miserable, guilty and ashamed. The motivation behind conviction is that God loves you and wants to help you become more like Christ. The motivation behind condemnation is that Satan hates your guts and wants to make you miserable. Conviction is specific, and condemnation is general. God will tell you what you did wrong and wants you to confess and repent of it. After you have confessed and have repented, then the conviction leaves instantly. Condemnation goes on and on for weeks or for years. Romans 8:1 states, "Therefore, there is now no condemnation for those who are in Christ Jesus." God never attacks my value. If you're hearing "You're worthless, you're hopeless, you're unlovable…" it's not from God, it's from Satan. Too many people, including Christians, mistake their own low self-esteem for the voice of God.

7. Do I sense God's peace about it? If you are feeling pressured, overwhelmed, or confused, then it's not from God. God wants us to sense His peace, not pressure. 1 Corinthians 14:33 says, "for God [who is the source of their prophesying] is not a God of confusion and disorder but of peace and order" (AMP).

CHAPTER 9 | BAGGAGE

(CONFESSING OUR SINS)

I became a Christian technically when I was in fourth grade. However, I didn't have a whole lot of biblical training or knowledge until after I graduated from college. I remember thinking that the only sins that one could commit were the ones listed in the Ten Commandments. Someone had asked me if I had sinned one day, and I'm embarrassed to say that I stated, "No" because I was thinking that if I hadn't committed any murders, or lied, or was envious of anyone, or had used the Lord's name in vain that day then I had not committed any sins. I have since learned that almost anything can become a sin. Our thought life, the way we gossip, the actions we don't take that we should, and our ulterior motives can all be considered sin. The more I grew as a Christian, the more I realized just how much I sinned. In fact, each of us sin each and every day, whether we want to believe it or not. Romans 3:23 states, "for all have sinned and fall short of the glory of God." And 1 John 1:8–10 states, "If we claim to be without sin, we deceive ourselves and the truth is not in us. If we confess our sins, He is faithful and just and will forgive us our sins and purify us from all unrighteousness. If we claim we have not sinned, we make Him out to be liar and His word has no place in our lives."

A few years ago, a woman at our church suggested that I go to a "Freedom in Christ" class that was offered at Bethel College. This wasn't a class for credit but was run by a missionary named Bill Jones who taught the class for just the cost of the materials. In this class we spent a weekend examining and then confessing all of the sins that had accumulated in us throughout our lives. We were to come with a partner to whom we could confess. Being a pastor's wife at the time, I didn't feel comfortable sharing my sins with anyone in my congregation (although I wish now that I would have), so my husband asked a Pentecostal woman he knew to be my partner. She was very conservative and seemed a little uncomfortable. I really wanted to take advantage of the opportunity to get all of my sins off my back, so I made sure I confessed everything that I was aware of at that time, which revealed many dark and hidden sins that I had covered up over the years. I think I scared this poor woman away by revealing all of my horrible sins, since she didn't come back after the first night! I was then paired up with Bill Jones's wife for the remainder of the class.

I learned a lot during that class, including how important it is to confess our sins with one another. Someone once told me, "We can confess our sins to God and be forgiven, but we can only claim victory over our sins when we confess our sins to another." James 5:16 says, "Therefore confess your sins to each other and pray for each other so that you may be healed. The prayer of a righteous man is powerful and effective." In other words, we become healed by confessing our sins to Christ to forgive you, by confessing our sins to one another, and by praying for each other. Don't you want to be healed? Aren't you tired of carrying around the dead weight of your sins? Look, we all sin. We just need to be honest about it. Don't you want victory over your sin? Or do you want to hide and act like you don't have a problem when you do? Proverbs 28:13 states, "He who conceals his sins does not prosper, but whoever confesses and renounces them finds mercy." We need to keep a short list with God and be able to be open and honest about our sins with others. Think about how much less we would sin if we knew we had to confess it to another person (although this in itself shouldn't be our motivation). I would encourage you to find someone of the same sex whom you can trust that you can be completely honest with and won't think of you any differently once they come to know all of your darkest sins. Once you find that person, meet at least once a month, or better yet, twice a month. It's hard and awkward at first, but will then become more normal. Confessing our sins to another causes us to become humble and God responds to humility.

I'm not sure why identifying and confessing our sins to one another or to God isn't practiced much today. Catholics confess their sins to their Priest as a regular part of their religious practices, although I believe it is better to confess to someone who can keep you more accountable. Protestants don't seem to be in the habit of confessing to one another at all, but only to God. Michael Mangis, who wrote a very interesting book called, *Signature Sins*, states, "Most congregations do not create a welcoming space for the confession of sin. Those in power often present themselves as icons of near-perfection. The common sinner, who cannot manage to hide sins so well, is left feeling inferior."[1] I do think today there are more and more pastors and priests that are opening up about their own sin and imperfections. However, I do agree that most congregations are not offering a space for the confession of sin with a fellow parishioner. Unless confession is modeled by the leaders of the church (within a safe place), I don't think confession will ever become commonplace within the church. That's sad, because in order to heal, we must confess "to one another." Healing will just become postponed, if it's addressed at all.

It's also just as important to confess our sins to God. When we confess our sins to God, we can ask Him to show us the root cause of our sin. If we don't ever discover the reasons why we are sinning in the first place, then chances are we will continue in the sin and feel self-defeated. We will begin to feel too embarrassed to share this with others and the hiding, as well as the sin, continues. Sometimes we become so attached to our sins, that we forget they are there. I think it is helpful to remember what sins are listed in the Bible, which are sometimes referred to as "The Seven Deadly sins." The seven deadly sins were first compiled by Pope Gregory I around the year 600. They are pride, greed, lust, wrath, gluttony, envy, and sloth. However, the list of seven deadly sins does not appear in any Bible verse. However, a slightly different set of sins can be found in Proverbs 6:16–19, "These six things the Lord hates, yes, seven are an abomination to Him:

1. a proud look,
2. a lying tongue,
3. hands that shed innocent blood,
4. a heart that devises wicked plans,
5. feet that are swift in running to evil,
6. a false witness who speaks lies,

and one who sows discord among brethren" (NKJ).

Look over the lists above and below and think about each of these areas when examining your thought life and actions. Here I've listed a more detailed list of the most common sins and a description of each, along with the coordinating virtue to pray for to replace that sin:

LUST

Sexual sins wound us more deeply than other sins because they strike at the core of the reflection of God's image of us. Men are more tempted visually, while women are more tempted by fantasies and stories through romance movies and novels.

The sin of lust has its root in the belief that God's love is not enough to satisfy our longing for intimacy.

Virtue to pray for: Moral Wholesomeness, Purity, Self-restraint

GLUTTONY

The pursuit and overindulgence of the body's appetites, especially for food and drink. It is not only about pleasure, but it is also used to escape

Virtue to pray for: Abstinence, Sobriety, Restraining Oneself from Indulging in Something

GREED

Grows out of suspicion that God will not take care of our needs as well as we can do it ourselves

Being over-driven to accumulate wealth, lust for power and status, waste-fullness or extravagance, stinginess, or by insisting having things done our way

Virtue to pray for: Unselfishness in Thought and in Action, Generousness, Open Heartedness

SLOTH

(Spiritual Apathy or Laziness) Comes from the distrust that God's goodness is sufficient to make the hard work of the spiritual life bear fruit and by refusing to receive and give grace.

Can look like being afraid of fighting for injustice, idleness, stubbornness, laziness in our responsibilities in any area of our life; complacency. Safety and comfort are important.

Virtue to pray for: Diligence, Budgeting one's time, Integrity, Zeal

ANGER (WRATH)

The sin of anger can cause more harm in our society that all other sins combined. All other sins can lead towards anger. Some of the root causes of anger can be injustice, strife, impatience, abuse of any kind, unmet needs, and jealousy.

Rage-aholics, Resentment, Quarrelsome, Assuming the worst in every situation, Vengeance, Paranoia, Groveling

Virtue to pray for: Patience, Forgiveness, Ability to Resolve Conflicts Peacefully, Show Mercy

ENVY

Dissatisfaction with who God has made me to be. It is also suspicion that God is withholding what I deserve and giving it to someone else.

Jealousy, Vindictive, Disrespectful

Virtue to pray for: Kindness, Admiration for others, Compassion, Sympathy, Friendship

PRIDE

The foundational sin—the desire to be like God.

Outward Pride: Narcissism, Vanity, Condescending, Disregard for Authority, Disobedience, Unrepentant

Inward Pride: Distrust, Perfectionism, Overly-Emotional, Over-Confident

Virtue to pray for: Humility, Selflessness, Giving Respect

I have never thought about the fact that certain personalities have certain sins in common with one another. In Michael Mangis' book, *Signature Sins*, he states, "Despite individual differences, human thought and behavior fall into identifiable patterns." He suggests taking an Enneagram personality test (which can be found easily on the internet) to assess which personality type you are. There are 9 different personality types, which can then also be paired with a wing (or sub-personality) to further define yourself. I would recommend first taking the exam, and then reading his book to then find out which sins are most common within that personality type. My whole family has taken this test, and I was very much surprised at how accurate the personality type is of me, my husband and of our kids. I am a 5 (Observer/Thinker/Investigator) with 4 wing (Romantic/Individualist/Artist). It was kind of fun to learn that I share this same personality with Albert Einstein and Thomas Jefferson. Mangis' description on my personality's sin was very accurate (you'll have to read the book to find out what they are!).

Sin Inventory

It's also important that once a month we also do a sin inventory with God. As King David has expressed, "Investigate my life, O God, find out everything about me; Cross-examine and test me, get a clear picture of what I'm about; See for yourself whether I've done anything wrong—then guide me on the road to eternal life" (MSG). Plan a time when you can be quiet and alone, with a notebook in hand. Ask yourself and God the following questions:

- Write down all known sins that you have committed. Then ask God to reveal sins that you have committed that you are unaware of. Ask God what the root causes of sins are. Sometimes we think we know why we have sinned, but we don't. It may be from something we were totally unaware of. Only God will have the answer, so it's important to seek His wisdom. If you don't address the root cause the sin will continue.
- Is there someone that you haven't forgiven? Is there a relationship that you are in that is currently suffering? Have you done all that you can to seek forgiveness from them and to restore the relationship? Have you said you are sorry for what you have done?
- Are there any idols that I have replaced God with? Is there anything in my life that over-occupies my time, energy or thoughts?
- Are there any lies that I am currently believing? If you're not sure, ask God to reveal those lies to you and ask Him to replace those lies with His truth.
- Is there anything in my life that is off-balanced? Am I spending too much time or effort in a particular area that is hurting my relationships with my family? Are there areas in my life that I need to spend more time and effort? To have a balanced life, we need to look at all areas of health: Emotional, Physical, Spiritual, Relational, and Mental. Is

there an area that I need to become healthier in? Are you full-filling your God-given purpose in life?

- Have I been 100% honest with God and with others in my life? Telling the truth is just one part of a healthy relationship. More importantly, we are to speak the truth in love at all times. We also need to be honest with ourselves and especially with God. God already knows the truth. We just need to acknowledge the truth about ourselves to Him.

To keep this list as short as possible, it is wise to keep a short account with God on a day-to-day basis. It is best to confess our sins right after we commit them.

A Few Words on Generational Sin

Do you find yourself asking, "Why am I sinning in this area, when I swore I would never struggle with this like my parents did?" If you have, that's generational sin. Michael Mangis states, "In my work as a therapist, I am amazed at the intricate ways in which family patterns of sin haunt people, even without their knowledge. I have seen individuals have an extramarital affair, only to learn afterwards that a parent had an affair at the same age. Many parents lament that they replicate the unhealthy habits of their own parents, despite all their promises to themselves that they would not repeat their parents' mistakes."[2]

Did you know that with generational sin, the feeling of shame or guilt from committing that sin doesn't get passed down? We wonder why we don't feel guilty or bad about what we've done. Sometimes this takes someone else pointing out the sin to us (like our spouse). That's why generational sin is so common today. In fact, most of us are still carrying around some sort of generational sin. When we don't acknowledge the sin or confess it, this generational sin will very likely continue onto your kids. That's why taking a sin inventory with God and then confessing it is important. Ask God how this sin can be stopped once and for all, so that your kids do not suffer from it.

Generational sin is one of those topics that is somewhat controversial. Some people believe that once you become a Christian, the devil (nor demons) no longer has any effect on us—this would include generational sin. Others believe that generational sin can only be removed with a "Deliverance Prayer." I believe something in between the two extreme views. I do think generational sin is more common and affects our lives much more often than we think it does. I also believe that we can, with God's help, overcome it. The Bible talks about generational sin in Exodus 20:5, Exodus 34:7 & Numbers 14:18, "… He punishes the children for the sin of the fathers to the third and fourth generation." But our hope is that God will also show love to a thousand generations of those who love Him and keep His commandments (Exodus 20:6).

In my own experience, I have noticed that when I am tempted in a particular area that my father has sinned, it is more difficult to resist than other temptations that I have faced. I have learned that the guilt of the sin doesn't get passed down. In fact, I would describe it as a stronghold. I also believe that when a particular sin is passed down to the next generation, that generation will have tendencies towards that particular sin, making it more difficult to resist. For instance, if your father was an alcoholic, you are not doomed to be an alcoholic as well, but if that sin was passed down to you, then you would become more likely to be addicted to alcohol as well. You do not have to give into the temptation, but you are more susceptible to fall in that area. However, whether we are more susceptible in an area or not, that should never become an excuse for falling into sin, no matter if it is generational sin or not.

When studying sin and temptation, I have learned that all of us are tempted at one time or another. In fact, in Matthew 18:7, it says, "Woe to the world for temptations to sin! **For it is necessary that temptations come**, but woe to the one by whom the temptation comes" (ESV) (Emphasis mine). However, keep in mind that God does not tempt us (James 1:13). Satan does. And God will not allow us to be tempted beyond what we can bear. He does provide a way out for us, even though we may need to suffer as we look for a way to escape. This may mean that we may need to quit our job, get rid of our computer or phone, or disassociate with our friends. It helps to remember that there is no new temptation under the sun. Christians have dealt with your particular struggle before and have overcame that same temptation. So, if they have overcome it, so can we. We are to watch (keep an eye out for) and pray that we don't fall into temptation (Matt 26:41, Mark 14:38), because "sin is crouching at your door" (Gen 4:7).

A well-known scripture verse regarding temptation is found in 1 Corinthians 10: 12–14, "So, if you think you are standing firm, be careful that you don't fall! No temptation has overtaken you except what is common to man. And God is faithful; He will not let you be tempted beyond what you can bear. But when you are tempted, He will also provide a way out so that you can stand up under it."

However, we often forget about the next verse which state, **"Therefore, my dear friends, flee from idolatry."** When we are tempted, we have placed something before God. This is idolatry. We are struggling between what we want (that we know God doesn't approve of) and God. Once we recognize it as idolatry, it helps us to treat it as so.

In Colossians 3:5 it states, "Put to death, therefore, whatever belongs to your earthly nature: sexual immorality, impurity, lust, evil desires and greed, **which is idolatry**" (emphasis mine). This verse also states that we are to "**put to death**" the sin in our lives. Colossians 3:8 continues, telling us to rid ourselves of anger, rage, vindictiveness, speaking falsely or unkind about others, and filthy language from our lips. We are not to lie. That means we are to eradicate, exterminate, execute or totally eliminate our sin so that it doesn't come back. Just like our literal "poo," or like an onset of cancer, we are to "**put to death**" and eliminate it entirely, so that it doesn't cause a more permanent infection. We then are to "**put on the new self**" or "**clothe ourselves with**" compassion, kindness, humility, gentleness and patience. We are to bear one another's burdens, and forgive each other. We are also to "**put on**" the virtue of Love, which binds us together in perfect unity.

One of the more interesting insights on temptation that I have learned is that temptation can actually be a good thing. James 1:2–3 states, **"Consider it pure joy, my brothers and sisters, whenever you face trials of many kinds, because you know that the testing of your faith develops perseverance."**

TRIAL => TESTING => PERSEVERANCE => MATURITY

TRIAL => TEMPTATION => SIN => DEATH

Remember how important it is to constantly interrogate our thoughts? Here's some advice about fleeing from temptation from BibleAnswers.ie:

> If you find yourself thinking evil thoughts, it is because you have cultivated this practice. You have learned to think this way. And you can unlearn what you have learned. As someone has said, "Habit overcomes habit." Paul tells us the kinds of things we should be thinking about: "Finally, brothers, whatever is true, whatever is noble, whatever is right, whatever is pure, whatever is lovely, whatever is admirable—if anything is excellent or praiseworthy—think about such things. Whatever you have learned or received or heard from me, or seen in me—put it into practice. And the God of peace will be with you." (Philippians 4:8–9) Paul says we must practise thinking about these things. And with practice it will become habit.[3]

I would also suggest following these steps to find freedom from generational sin as well as any demonic influence in your life:

1. Surrender your control and your situation over to God (be specific).
2. Confess your sins to God (be specific).
3. Confess all known sins of your parents to God (be specific).
4. Pray that God would reveal to you any unknown sins that you are unaware of (sins that you have committed and the sins that your parents have committed).
5. Forgive your parents for their sins.

6. Ask God to break any ungodly soul ties, curses or generational sin with the sinning parent.

7. Ask God to break any demonic influences that have occurred.

The following is great example of the effects of generational blessing vs. generational sin:

America's greatest theologian, Jonathan Edwards and his wife Sarah had eleven children. Despite a rigorous work schedule that included rising as early as 4:30 a.m. to read and write in his library, extensive travels, and endless administrative meetings, he always made time for his children.

Indeed, he committed to spending at least one hour a day with them. And if he missed a day because he was traveling, he diligently made up the hour when he returned.

One scholar decided to chart the 1,394 known descendants of Edwards. What he found was an incredible testament to Johnathan Edwards. Of his known descendants there were 13 college presidents, 65 college professors, 30 judges, 100 lawyers, 60 physicians, 75 army and navy officers, 100 pastors, 60 authors of prominence, 3 United States senators, 80 public servants including governors, ministers to foreign countries and one vice-president of the United States.

The story of Jonathan Edwards is an example of what some sociologists call the "five-generation rule." But the five-generation rule works both ways.

Consider the case of Max Jukes, a contemporary of Edwards. As an adult, Jukes had a drinking problem that kept him from holding a steady job. It also kept him from showing much concern for his wife and children. He would disappear sometimes for days and return drunk and made little time for loving and instructing his children.

Of Jukes' known descendants, 310 died as paupers, at least 150 were criminals (including 7 murderers), more than 100 were drunkards and half of his female descendants ended up as prostitutes.[4]

PHASE THREE SUMMARY AND DISCUSSION QUESTIONS

PHASE THREE SUMMARY:

L = <u>Letting Go</u>
- Confronting your fear of healing.
- Learning why prayer is important and why we need to make it become a larger part of our lives.
- Confessing your sins, and learning about generational sin.

DISCUSSION QUESTIONS:

1. Did you have any fears before entering into the healing process? If so, what were they?

2. Are you committed to going through the steps to become emotionally healthy and then maintaining your emotional health? Why or why not?

3. Have you ever had a conversation with God before? If so, what was it like? If you haven't, why do you think you never have?

4. What are some things you can begin to do or change in your life that will allow you to spend more time in prayer and listening to God?

5. What are some questions or fears that you may have about having a conversation with God?

6. Have you ever confessed your sins to someone other than God? If so, what was it like? If not, why haven't you? How can this become a larger part of your life?

7. What are some things you learned about generational sin? Do you think you have generational sin? If so (and you don't mind sharing), what do you think that is?

8. Was the list of types of sins helpful to you? Was there anything on the sin list that surprised you that it was listed as a sin?

PRAYER TIME:

Ask God to take away any fear that you may have regarding beginning the steps to become emotionally healthy.

Ask God to begin speaking to you. Ask Him a question that you would like Him to answer, then wait for a response from Him.

Ask God to show you who may be a good person to become an accountability partner with.

When you are by yourself, ask God to forgive you of your sins, by listing all known sins and then ask Him to reveal to you any sins that you are unaware of.

PHASE 4: ALLOWING GOD THE OPPORTUNITY TO HEAL US

Developing Emotionally Healthy Habits by Exercising Our Emotions

If you happened to have watched the movie Groundhog Day (1993), you'd find that the main character, Phil Connors (played by Bill Murray), is stuck repeating the same day over and over again and he's the only one who realizes it. In order to become "unstuck," Phil must redeem himself with the world. He must learn to make the most of the day and spend it on helping others in order for the universe to be appeased and for him to once again live life one day after another. While repeating the same day, Phil learns how to play the piano, learns to speak French and memorize French poetry, helps out the whole town with various problems that arise, and finally wins the heart of his female co-worker (played by Andie MacDowell).

Did you know that someone actually figured out how long it would take to learn and do all of the things that Phil did? They calculated that it would have taken about 33 years and 350 days living the same day over and over to have learned the things Phil learned while he was courting Rita. It takes over 4,000 days just to learn French.

We can very easily become stuck too. Stuck in our unbiblical thought life, stuck in our self-defeating endeavors, stuck in our relationships, stuck in our marriage, or just plain stuck! According to Rick Warren we get stuck when we don't release our grievances. So, in order to become unstuck, we need to take an inventory of our lives and discover where we haven't grieved over the losses we've experienced. When we don't grieve, we stay stuck emotionally at the age when the event happened. Kevin and I have seen many "stuck" people throughout our ministry. We once knew a guy who was a strong Christian but was pretty immature. After getting to know him, we found out that his dad had died when he was just 18 years old. Since he never fully grieved, he remained at that age emotionally. As John Piper has stated "Occasionally, weep deeply over the life you hoped would be. Grieve the losses. Then wash your face. Trust God. And embrace the life you have."

A Brief History of Grieving

The Bible uses different words to describe grief: lamenting, weeping, wailing, moaning, grieving, and mourning, to name a few. There are over 430 verses that incorporate these words in the Bible that reflect the importance of grieving. There's even a whole book of the Bible called Lamentations (the word "lamentation" means a passionate expression of grief or sorrow). We've lost the ability to know how to grieve and God's original plan for it. Grieving was an outward expression from the result of being brought low or reduced in stature, mourning and/or repentance. In biblical times, grief was expressed freely and began immediately. Those who grieved tore their clothes, and at times tore out their hair, sprinkled ashes on their heads, removed all jewelry, fasted, and wept as an outward expression of their grief. Someone wanting to show his repentant heart would often wear sackcloth, sit in ashes, and put ashes on top of their head.

Sackcloth and ashes were used to symbolically display the condition of someone's heart. Sackcloth was a coarse material usually made of goat's hair, making it very uncomfortable to wear. The ashes represented desolation and ruin. When someone died, the act of putting on sackcloth showed sorrow for the loss of their loved one. When referring to mourning for the dead, sackcloth is usually mentioned, but not ashes. Ashes usually were associated with sackcloth when there was a national disaster or repenting of sin. Sackcloth and ashes were also used as a public sign of repentance and humility before God. The period of grieving would last as short as seven days (for someone they may not have known well), to as long as thirty (for their loved ones).

What really bothers me about our society today is that we are no longer grieving. At least in biblical times, it was considered "normal" to outwardly express our grief. By putting on sackcloth, people knew that others were hurting just by looking at them and could help console them. It was common for people to "wail" and "groan" for their losses, while their friends joined in. It was also common for others to just sit with their hurting friends, like in the case of Job. They didn't have to say anything, but their friends felt their concern and love for them because they were there. Today we are not able to tell if someone is hurting because we tend to "put on a good face" when we really are deeply hurting inside. We are usually only given just three days off from work for a loved one's funeral. That isn't nearly enough time to grieve as we need to. We go back to work three days later and put on our happy face again and hide away our pain.

And why do we only acknowledge time off (or time dedicated for grieving) for funerals, when there are thousands of other reasons we may be suffering and need time to grieve? Maybe you just went through a divorce, or maybe your child has cancer, or maybe you're still trying to cope from being molested as a child. The point is, we need to grieve. It's imperative for our emotional, spiritual, physical and mental health. And it is imperative that we learn HOW to grieve. If there is something that you have never grieved over, you need to grieve now before it continues to affect your life. If you take the time to review your life, I bet you have had several difficult moments in your life that you've never grieved over, if not more. If you have not grieved, then you are repressing or suppressing (stuffing) your emotions which will lead to it coming out in some way, either causing damage to your body or damaging others in your reaction to them. If you have never grieved over your losses, you will more than likely stay stuck emotionally at the age when the pain occurred.

So, in order to become unstuck, we need to first take an inventory of our lives and discover where we haven't grieved over the losses that we've experienced. Then, we need to identify what we've really lost. Maybe in the man's life mentioned earlier who's dad died when he was young, the real loss was that he missed out on years of encouragement and guidance from his dad, or that he would never get the opportunity for his kids to get to know his father. There are many real loses that we've experienced throughout our lives that we've never taken the time to acknowledge. Don't rush through this stage but take the time to list each of these losses. If you are having trouble identifying what the real losses are, ask God to show you. Then write them down as they come to mind.

Once we have made a list of our real losses, then we need to lament to God. When talking about lamenting, Rick Warren has stated, "We as Christians know how to praise God and to make our requests known to God, but we don't know how to lament. Lamenting is a passionate expression of grief to God…this can include complaining."

The thought of crying out to God with all of our emotional pain sure doesn't sound like fun, but it's necessary. Some people never enter into healing because they don't want to enter into the pain again. They are afraid that they won't ever stop crying, or that they will never stop hurting. But let me assure you that you will.

Shortly before Kevin and I got married, I allowed myself to finally weep over my parents' divorce. I had bought a workbook that helped worked through the pain from divorce so that I could finally deal with the hurt that I had still felt. I had stuffed it for so long, I thought that if I began to cry I wouldn't stop. When I finally began to let go and begin to cry, I wept for three days straight. I didn't realize how much pain had built up and how much it had affected me. I knew releasing this pain was important because I didn't want to bring this pain (poo) into our marriage.

We are also fearful that God will be mad at us if we complain to Him or will punish us somehow. But that is a lie. God loves when we come to Him with our pain. In the book of Psalms, King David often went to God in his distress and pain. In Psalm 5:1–2 David cries, "Give ear to my words, O Lord, consider my sighing. Listen to my cry for help, my King and my God, for to You I pray." When David was fleeing from his son Absalom, he cried out, "I was crying to the Lord with my voice, and He answered me from His holy mountain. I lay down and slept; I awoke, for the Lord sustains me." In this verse, David was able to sleep after God answered his cry while his enemies were chasing him. God also wants to answer you and give you peace as you cry out to Him.

When I have been the most frustrated with my life, I have cried out to God. He has always heard me, encouraged me and has given me hope. Those intimate experiences with God have changed my life. I just need to remember to go to God every time I feel that way. Wouldn't you rather have your child or your spouse come to you with their hurts than for them to complain to others about you?

So, how do we lament? We cry out to God. We tell Him exactly what we are angry about or why we are hurting. We can scream, cry, whine, get snotty, confess, and pour out of hearts to God. Because God can take it... really. And believe it or not, when we express our deepest emotions to God, we will draw even closer to Him. Don't you draw closer to others when you share your emotions with others and they don't judge you for it? It's the same with our relationship with God.

With these bible verses, we can turn to God's word for ease and comfort as we grieve:

- "He will wipe every tear from their eyes. There will be no death' or mourning or crying or pain, for the old order of things has passed away" (Rev. 21:4).

- "The Lord is close to the brokenhearted and saves those who are crushed in spirit" (Psalm 34:18).
- "He heals the brokenhearted and binds up their wounds" (Psalm 147:3).
- "Do not let your hearts be troubled. Trust in God; trust also in me" (John 14:1).
- "Surely He took up our pain and bore our suffering, yet we considered Him punished by God, stricken by Him, and afflicted. But He was pierced for our transgressions, He was crushed for our iniquities; the punishment that brought us peace was on Him, and by His wounds we are healed. We all, like sheep, have gone astray, each of us has turned to our own way; and the Lord has laid on Him the iniquity of us all" (NIV Isaiah 53:4–6).
- "Blessed are those who mourn, for they will be comforted" (Matthew 5:4).
- "Praise be to the God and Father of our Lord Jesus Christ, the Father of compassion and the God of all comfort, who comforts us in all our troubles, so that we can comfort those in any trouble with the comfort we ourselves have received from God. For just as the sufferings of Christ flow over into our lives, so also through Christ our comfort flows. If we are distressed, it is for your comfort and salvation; if we are comforted, it is for your comfort, which produces in you patient endurance of the same sufferings we suffer. And our hope for you is firm, because we know that just as you share in our sufferings, so also you share in our comfort" (2 Cor. 1:3–7).

CHAPTER 11 | THE EAGLE

(CONVERSING WITH GOD)

I recently received an email describing what an eagle goes through during its' life. I never knew that even though eagles can live for up to 70 years, they have to undergo a very painful experience in order to reach that age. At the age of 40 years old, the eagle has two options: die or undergo major transformation that will allow it to live for another 30 years. At the age of 40, the eagle's long and flexible talons can no longer grab prey which serves as food. It's long and sharp beak becomes bent. It's old-aged and heavy wings, due to their thick feathers, become stuck to its' chest and make it difficult to fly. They must undergo transformation that will last 150 days in order to survive. The process requires that the eagle fly to a mountain top and sit on its' nest. The eagle will then knock its' beak against a rock until it plucks it out. After plucking it out, the eagle will wait for a new beak to grow back and then it will pluck out its' talons (claws). When the talons grow back, the eagle starts plucking its' old-aged feathers. And after five months, the eagle takes its' famous flight of rebirth and is able to live for thirty more years.

I don't know about you, but if I was an eagle, I sure wouldn't want to hit my head against a rock to destroy and then pluck out my own beak, nor my claws, nor my feathers. Sounds too painful… sounds too crazy. But to survive, it must. And in order for us to survive, or live the fullest life God intended us to, we must do some plucking to ourselves as well.

How do we know we need plucking? Anytime you over-react to something (which we ALL do at some point or another). In Galatians 5:22–23 it says, "But the fruit of the Spirit [the result of His presence within us] is love [unselfish concern for others], joy, [inner] peace, patience [not the ability to wait, but how we act while waiting], kindness, goodness, faithfulness, gentleness, and self-control." These feelings and character traits should come natural to us and not become just something to strive for. So, if we are not experiencing these feelings, then we should know that something is wrong.

I look back on my life and recognize that for many years I had experienced so many negative emotions: I was worried, stressed, afraid or impatient. I had anxiety, or was angry, sad, or lonely. Emotions are kind of like a "check engine light" that goes on in your car letting you know that even though your car may be running ok for now, it soon might not be unless we get it checked by our local mechanic soon. Feelings like worry and fear are warning signs telling us that we need to pay attention to our spiritual and emotional well-being as well as our thought life.

Like most of us, I wasn't taught how to handle my emotions or how to recognize them as warning signs. Not being brought up in a Christian home, I didn't learn how to take my concerns to God. Instead, I stuffed them deep inside so that no one would know that they were there and so that I could then go back to my "so-called" happy life. We think that eventually the pain will go away by itself, but it doesn't. We seek other relationships to help mask the pain. We find ways to distract ourselves and dull our senses. We push the self-defeating thoughts away. We talk to our friends, thinking they'll help us to feel better about ourselves, or we become inclusive so that no one else can hurt us.

A couple of years ago, we had a couple of men that stayed with us who were from Africa. They were in town for a local prayer event that my husband had organized. Both were missionaries that were employed by "Youth with a Mission," or YWAM for short. We got on the subject of inner healing, and they mentioned that they have seen and have experienced great success in inner healing through using a method called, "Theophostic Prayer (Now called Transformational Prayer Ministry)," based out of Tennessee. So I got on Amazon and ordered the book called, *Healing Life Hurts Through Theophostic Prayer* by Edward M. Smith. I was blown away by what I read. I was so impressed, that about a year later, my husband and I went to one of Edward Smith's conferences for training. If you are interested in learning more about his ministry, I would highly recommend that you take a look at his new website (which also includes free training): www.transformationprayer.org.

What I took away from the information that we learned from the conference, as well as the insightful book, is just how important our feelings are and why it's so important to find out what lies we have believed that are causing those emotions. We need to recognize our negative emotions as a way of God telling us that there is something wrong that needs His healing. According to Ed Smith, this is caused by an event or a word that has been said to us usually between the ages of 3–12. A lie becomes attached to that event and becomes difficult to recognize or to let go of, without God's help. There's actually evidence that when we have thoughts during a traumatic event, those thoughts become literally "embedded" into our brain. The devil is smart and knows that if he can embed a lie within us that will affect the rest of our lives, he will.

In an online article entitled. "Bad Memories Stick Better than Good" by Andrea, Thompson, it states, "Our brains have a specific memory network that kicks into gear whenever we are trying to remember something,' author Elizabeth Kensinger of Boston College told LiveScience. 'But it seems like when we're having an emotional reaction, the emotional circuitry in the brain kind of turns on and enhances the processing in that typical memory network such that it works even more efficiently and even more effectively to allow us to learn and encode those aspects that are really relevant to the emotions that we're experiencing.'"[1] So, in other words, when we have any kind of an emotional experience (especially negative ones), we not only remember that experience more vividly than other memories, but many times, the devil will place within our minds a lie that becomes attached to that event.

These lies affect our way of thinking about life and how we respond to the relationships that are around us. If a young girl grows up with a harsh father, she may believe the lie that states that "all men are bad." Think about how this lie would affect all the relationships she has with men throughout the rest of her life, including a possible future husband. If you have a lie implanted within you while you were molested as a child, you may grow up believing the lie that it was your fault. This lie would then affect how you might become susceptible to become involved in relationships that are co-dependent, by making excuses for others' wrong behavior and by enabling those around you. Perhaps you have believed the lie that you will never be good, pretty, or smart enough, or that no one will ever love you. Some people will believe the lie that everyone is thinking bad thoughts about them, so when someone is talking to them, they immediately think that any statement the person makes (regardless of who they are talking about) that they are really referring to them and they take it personally. Lies like this can be so damaging to the relationships of those around them. Everyone's lie may be different, so it's important to ask God what those lies are, so that they can be replaced with the truth so that it will not continue to affect our lives. I personally believe that everyone has lies that they have come to believe, just some have more than others. We cannot be healed just through intellectual means. We must have an experience (a conversation, impression or vision) with Christ in order to heal.

Now, I'm not going to go through the steps of "Theophostic" or "Transformational Prayer" with you (for that you can visit Dr. Ed Smith's website: www.transformationprayer.org), but I am going to show you a simpler set of steps that I have taken for my own personal inner healing, that I'll call simply, "Listening to God." Instead of using a particular set of questions to move me along with exposing the lies and the truth, as in the methods used in "Transformational Prayer," I have more of a conversation with God. I've found that by having a conversation with God, God usually reveals to me much more detail than I probably would have received otherwise. My passion is to share and teach these steps with others.

So, get ready, here are the steps:

1. Find time to be alone with God when there won't be any distractions (maybe lock yourself in the bathroom if you have kids!).

2. Identify the negative feeling that is most preoccupying your life at this time. Be as specific as possible. Here's a short list of possible negative emotions for help: Abandoned, Afraid, Annoyed, Angry, Anxious, Betrayed, Confused, Defensive, Depressed, Distracted, Disturbed, Disgusted, Disappointed, Envious, Fearful, Frustrated, Guilty, Grieved, Hopeless, Offended, Overwhelmed, Pessimistic, Prideful, Regretful, Resentful, Sad, Self-Pity, Shame, Stressed, Troubled, Upset, Uncomfortable, Unhappy, Victimized, Vulnerable, Worried

3. Cry out to God. Tell Him in detail what you are feeling. Ask Him to take you back to the first time that you felt that feeling (usually between the ages of 3 and 12). Usually you will begin to feel that feeling again once you have remembered that event.

4. Ask God to show you the lie that became attached to that event.

5. Then ask God to show you the truth (His truth) to replace the lie.

6. Take time to be open with God, allowing Him to show you all that He has for you. Sometimes this process can last a few minutes but can last much longer.

7. This process is continual and needs to become a habit. Each time we overreact, we need to do this process again, throughout the rest of our lives.

To further illustrate these steps, I'll share a few examples from my own "Listening to God" experiences.

1st example: The first time I knowingly tried "Listening to God" was during the Theophostic conference that I was learning it from. We had gotten back to our hotel, and I thought I was hungry. Then I had realized that I had become attached to food in an unhealthy way. I had to bring food with me whenever we went anywhere. I think it began when I had to start packing a diaper bag when my kids were first born. I always had a change of clothes, diapers, wipes, toys and food with us whenever we went out. However, I continued to pack food, even after my kids got older. Whether it was going for a hike, or for a car ride, traveling or just going to someone else's house, I always had food with us. I then realized that I was associating food with comfort. So, I asked God when this association began, and He showed me many of the family get-togethers we have had throughout the years. Of course, like many family get-togethers, those times were surrounded by food. "What was the main course?" What were we bringing?" "How much should we make?" I noticed that the meals themselves were the event. Socializing was something we did while we were waiting for the food to be ready, during the meal and immediately after. Once I realized that I had been thinking more about the food than the socializing, I knew I had believed the lie that it was the food that comforted me, and not the people surrounding me. Once God revealed that lie to me, I felt a different association with food from that point on. Food is something to be enjoyed, but I now knew that it would not comfort me. I no longer had the urge to pack food with us when we went out from that point on. I still pack food occasionally when we are on a long trip, but I don't sense the unhealthy connection with food as I once had.

2nd example: Not too long ago, a good friend a mine at work was kidding around and before he left to go home for the day, he jokingly stated that he was going to "go home and beat his wife" (which he would never do). I immediately became upset and said, "Please don't say that, because it's not funny." That statement triggered a very emotionally negative response from me, and it was difficult to continue to work without crying. At first, I knew what he said was morally wrong (even though I knew he was kidding) but I didn't understand why I had such a strong emotional reaction to that statement. I then remembered that a few years earlier Kevin and I had gotten into a huge fight. The fight had gotten so bad, that I went into another room to end the conversation and to be away from Kevin. Kevin followed me and was extremely angry. When I saw him approaching me I started to cower, by putting up my hands thinking that he would strike me. Kevin then calmed down and we separated the rest of the evening. He later told me that when he saw my hands go up to protect myself that he knew he went over board and began to ask God why he had become so angry. God brought him back to a time when he was around 8 years old and was playing with the neighborhood kids. These kids taunted him and told him he had to "physically pleasure" the older boys in a very inappropriate way or that they would beat him up. Kevin said he felt very unprotected and vulnerable that day and knew that that incident was causing his anger today. God has since healed him from that incident.

I honestly felt the same way. I felt very unprotected and vulnerable and I knew that there was nothing that I could have done to protect myself, since he was so much stronger than me. I actually had a thought that ran across my mind that said, "I get it. I get why women become lesbians because no woman ever wants to experience this in her life again" (*more on this subject in my next book*). I told Kevin about my reaction to my coworker that evening and cried for what seemed like an eternity. I did, however, realize the next day that it was that time of month when I tend to become much more emotional. However, I still believe that all emotions are God's way of telling us that there is something wrong that needs to heal within us. It's just that some days we (us women) may become more emotional than others (yes girls, we do need to admit that!). But I also had to admit just how impactful that one incident was to my emotional well-being and how much hurt was still there. I had never processed or tried to heal from that experience. It felt good to finally release the pain I had within me and I felt that I could now begin to heal. Kevin laid next to me as I cried. He promised that he would never strike me and that I could trust him. I was so glad to finally confront and begin to heal that ugly part of our lives. My co-worker friend also apologized for joking about that subject, once he saw my reaction and stated that he would never joke about that again.

3rd example: A few years ago, I was feeling overwhelmingly lonely. As I was having my own pity-party, I thought about my best friend moving away and how much I've missed her, that we are now going to a much larger church where it can take time to connect with other women, and how I am the only woman in the engineering department where I work with over thirty men. I cried out to God, asking Him to show me the first time I felt overwhelmingly lonely. He brought to my mind a series of events that happened during my freshman year of high school. My mother and father had just remarried (to other people), my step-dad had recently moved in, and my only sibling, my brother

Randy, had just left for college. I didn't have anyone in my life at the time to talk to about what I was going through. I remember being lonely and depressed for weeks and had written in my journal several times that I wanted to die. My mother had found and read my journal and began worrying about me, so she took me to get checked out at a local psychiatric treatment center. I was interviewed by a doctor who then told my mother that I was "normal," and that I didn't need any additional care. However, a couple of weeks later, I looked around the house to see if there were any pills that I could take so that I could overdose. Fortunately, the only pills I found were aspirin. I opened the bottle and took most of the entire bottle and went to bed. To my surprise, I woke up the next day feeling a little groggy, but otherwise was perfectly fine. No one ever knew. I think I had a thought like, "I can even screw this up." Looking back at that time of my life, I think I just wanted some attention. I felt lonely, overlooked, and was unpopular at school.

While thinking through my past, the feeling of loneliness came back to me with the same intensity that I felt as I had written several times in my diary that I wanted to die. I asked God to show me the lie I had believed and he revealed to me the lie that I thought I was alone. He then showed me that I wasn't alone, and that I had never been alone. Even though I didn't have a close relationship with God at the time, He showed me all the ways He had been there for me throughout the years of my youth. The times He had saved me from car wrecks and kept me safe in so many ways—especially during my college years. He showed me how He listened to and had answered my prayers throughout my life. He showed me how He had answered my prayers for a husband, to become a mom when it appeared as though I was barren, and the time I had prayed for a best friend and was blessed by her for many years before she moved away. He even showed me many answers to prayer for smaller things too… jobs that He had provided, and the many people in my life that I have been blessed by. He then opened my eyes to others that I knew who were much more alone than I was—widows and singles and those whose kids have moved out of the house. He reminded me that I had kids and a husband who really loved me at home. Well, needless to say, I didn't feel lonely anymore. I felt a lot of the burden and hurt leave me at that moment, and for the most part, they have not come back.

#4 example: After about twenty years of attending our church, we were approached by another church to merge with one another. After a few months into the merger we started noticing some red flags. On the outside, the merger appeared to go well, but behind the scenes it didn't. I began to feel very angry towards this pastor. But I had considered him a friend, and I didn't want to continue to be angry with him. I asked God to show me why I was angry. I then remembered that during the Theophostic training we were told that when it came to anger, we needed to identify the true feeling that was causing the anger. So, after much thought I was able to discern that I felt hurt by someone I should have been able to trust. I brought this feeling to God and I asked Him to reveal to me the first time I had felt hurt by someone I should have been able to trust. He brought me back to when I was about 3–5 years old when my father was just returning from a weekend of being away on a "business trip." When my dad came into the door, I wrapped by arms around his leg so that he had to walk with me hanging onto him. He then was apparently annoyed with me and shook me off his leg. I felt crushed. God then revealed to me the lie that I began to believe, "My dad doesn't love me." God said that that was a lie, and that indeed, my dad did love me. God explained to me that my dad was feeling ashamed because he had just come in from a weekend of having an affair, and that that was the reason he shook me from his leg. Immediately, a lot of the hurt that I had felt towards my dad was healed. I now knew that he loved me. At the same time, I also no longer had any anger towards this pastor. It was amazing to me how instantly and how permanently this healing was that God had given me.

I still have more healing to pursue, because each and every hurt that we've experience throughout our lives needs to be addressed separately. I know I still need additional healing because I still over-react to things, but not nearly as often now since I began following these steps. God is good! I would encourage you to follow these steps as well. These experiences that I have had with God have transformed my life and they will also transform yours as well.

CHAPTER 12 | HOW AMERICANS ARE ESCAPING FROM LIFE

(HEALING OUR MARRIAGES)

There is a colossal amount of people who are so unfulfilled with everyday life, that they need a way (seemingly anyway) to escape from how they feel. At heart what drives any compulsive form of escapism is temporary relief from pain—be it physical, emotional, mental or spiritual.[1]

Escapism is probably the area that I have struggled with most in my life. A couple of years ago I met someone that I felt I really connected with (we'll call him Friendly Fred for privacy sake). My husband and I had had problems in our marriage for years, and it was continually becoming worse. I would share with Friendly Fred my problems as well as many other aspects of my life. I felt I could tell him anything. Over time, I grew to really care about Friendly Fred and eventually asked to meet with him to let him know that I had developed feelings for him. Fortunately, when we met to talk, Friendly Fred stated that he saw me just as a friend, and then asked what was going on in my marriage. I told him about the fights I had had with my spouse and that it was becoming very difficult to talk to him about anything. Friendly Fred said he'd be praying for me and we remained good friends. That next day, I cried out to God. It was probably the most intense conversation I've ever had with God, let alone anyone else. I told Him that I was very frustrated and unhappy. I poured out my heart to Him in tears. I told Him

I so desperately wanted not just an "OK" marriage, but that I wanted a great marriage, but didn't know how that could happen. God then told me that he loved me and that someday I would indeed, have that kind of marriage. I just needed to trust in Him. He said that for now He had given me Friendly Fred as a good friend to help me get through it. I walked away from the conversation believing in that promise, but I just didn't know how or when He would fulfill it. To be honest with you, there were many days that I would begin to doubt and would think that it just wouldn't happen.

After hearing that promise from God, my feelings for Fred should have ended, but they didn't. I continued to fantasize about Friendly Fred, which took on a life of its own. At that point, it wasn't that our relationship got any closer, but my fantasies were becoming more and more frequent and more intense. I liked the feelings my fantasy life provided for me and I liked escaping. Eventually, however, I felt like my feelings and my fantasies were becoming out of my control and that it was beginning to affect other areas of my life, so I decided that I really needed to confess these thoughts to someone who could keep me accountable. I met a woman that I deeply respected who I knew had a heart for counseling other women.

When we met I confessed everything to her. I think she was a little shocked at just how open and graphic I was about the thoughts I'd been having. She said that she would help me keep me accountable and we began meeting with each other. At times she would become frustrated with me for not having any remorse over my sin. I told her that I had constantly been studying scripture, listening to sermons, and praying, but that nothing seemed to help me to grieve over my sin. I realize now that I had no remorse because this was a generational sin that I had inherited from my father. My dad had on-going affairs from the time I was in kindergarten to the time he left my mother and our family when I was 15. I knew I didn't want this sin to be passed down to my kids.[2]

My accountability partner eventually challenged me to tell Kevin about Friendly Fred. I reluctantly did sometime later. I knew I had hurt him over the years as well, and I didn't want to hurt him any further. It was very difficult, but I knew it was the right thing to do. Kevin initially responded by admitting that he had been unhappy with our relationship over the last year, and we decided to work on rebuilding our marriage. Kevin asked if I would begin meeting with him every Saturday morning to begin working through our problems and our hurts, which was really the best thing we could have done to save our marriage. Sometimes our talks went well, and sometimes it didn't, but it was worth it. I still had a lot of hurt that had built up over the years that I confessed to Kevin and he began to respond with compassion, instead of anger as he had before. It was at times messy, difficult and tiring, but it also helped to restore the trust and respect of him that I had lost.

I once heard that marriages get better by healing the inner pain within each person. I can tell you first-hand just how true that statement is. Kevin and I had brought into our marriage a lot of hurt that we both experienced while growing up. That pain altered our reality of our relationship and the way we viewed each other. It was only when we both began to receive inner healing, that our marriage became healthier. When our inner pain began to heal, we no longer could accuse the other person of causing that pain, because we realized that the pain was initially caused by the hurts we had experienced while growing up.

I can't say that my struggle with the temptation of fantasizing as a means to escape is completely gone, but I have come to understand that for some reason God has allowed me to experience this so that perhaps I can understand others who are going through the same thing. Even in Christian marriages, one half end up in divorce. However, just because you may be struggling in this area, doesn't mean that you can't overcome it. Look over Chapter 9 regarding sin and study ways the Bible has taught us to overcome temptation. However, sometimes the struggle remains, no matter what we do to try to resist it. Three times Paul asked God to remove his "thorn in his flesh" and three times God decided not to remove it. I think sometimes our struggles are meant for us to depend on God's guidance and strength each day. Each day as we face life, we need to just make the next right decision. As each day goes by, the right decision becomes easier.

There are many reasons why people say they get divorced. Some have said that it's because they "made a mistake" and cheated on their spouse. Some say that they fell out of love, or that they haven't been in love with their spouse for years. Dr. Craig L. Blomberg, a professor of New Testament at Denver Seminary, states, "In a country in which even many Christians think the pursuit of happiness is an inalienable right (no, just because The Declaration of Independence declares it so doesn't make it true), is it any wonder that people justify leaving their spouses because they just don't feel good anymore?" We are forgetting that biblical love (the same love we vowed directly to our spouse on our wedding day), is based on commitment and God's commands, and not our emotions. When we decide to divorce, we are, in essence, reneging on our wedding vows. Feelings change, but commitments should not.

When Kevin and I were going to pre-marriage counseling, our Pastor asked us, "Do you think that there is only one person in this world that would make the best spouse for you?" We answered "Yes." Then he gave us some advice that I have thought back on frequently during this time in our marriage. He said, "The truth is, there may be several people that we will meet in our life that might make us a good spouse." After several years of marriage, our Pastor had met someone that he became attracted to. He said he just had to keep in mind, that even though there was an attraction with another woman, he still was committed to his wife. They still have a happy marriage today.

I think sometimes it's easy for us to think that the grass is greener on the other side, and that other people have better relationship than ours. But I wish someone would have explained to me early on in my life that all relationships struggle to some degree. Not only is it normal, it's natural. All relationships have good and bad days. That doesn't mean that your relationship is not what God intended. God gives us people around us to help us grow emotionally and spiritually. Without conflict we won't grow or mature. The important question to ask is not: What can I do to get out of this relationship? or How can I change this other person? The question to God should be: What do you want me to learn from this conflict? or What do I need to change within myself or say to the other person to make this relationship better?

Kevin and I are still very much the same as we were when we initially began having problems, but the difference is that we now talk through the issues that had kept us distant before and don't let the negative feelings fester. We need to also remember the good experiences we've had throughout our marriage, and to keep those memories alive. It also helps me to concentrate on Kevin's wonderful qualities instead of his weaknesses... because we all have weaknesses. He has been so supportive of me while I've been writing this book, which has taken a great deal of my time. Kevin has willingly taken over the household chores and has allowed me the time I have needed to complete this mounting task. He is a fantastic father. He is even becoming a good cook! I also know that no other person in this world could love me as much as he does.

Our marriage today still isn't perfect. Nor will it ever be (or anyone else's). But we are beginning to rebuild what had been lost through the years and can begin to look forward to a bright future together. I now can believe that our marriage is becoming great, just as God had promised.

If you have been divorced, please keep in mind that God is full of grace and compassion. He can and will restore you if you allow Him to. But we also need to admit when we have sinned. We get so caught up in what our spouses have done to us that we forget that it's a two-way street. Instead of focusing on how much our spouse needs to change, we need to take a good, hard look at ourselves first. Matthew 7:1–5 states, "Do not judge, or you too will be judged. For in the same way your judge others, you will be judged, and with the measure you use, it will be measured to you. Why do you look at the speck of sawdust in your brother's eye and pay no attention to the plank in your own eye? How can you say to your bother, "Let me take the speck out of your eye, when all the time there is a plank in your own eye? You hypocrite, first take the plank out of your own eye, and then you will see clearly to remove the speck from your brother's eye."

Many times, I think we tend to want to avoid fixing our relationships and will instead escape in some way emotionally. It's easier and a lot more fun. We would rather watch TV, read a romance novel, or go shopping to make us feel better and avoid any uncomfortable relationships we may have. But the truth is, we need to work on our relationships and not escape from them.

While working on this book, I was doing research on different book genres and how much each genre sold. I was really surprised to discover that the largest book selling market was romance and erotic novels (at about 34% of the U.S. fiction market). Looking at some of the books online, I was shocked to discover how graphic some of these covers were... almost all had a guy with his shirt off or almost completely off, so that you can see his very buff body and six pack abs. The women had long, flowing hair and large breasts. It was almost like looking at soft porn. I realized that this is what many women have now turned to for escape. The average woman reads 1 romance novel a week. Reading romance novels and fantasizing about other men is an escape that many women use, even if we refuse to admit it. It does us no good to try to escape our pain. It actually only makes matters worse. The only way that pain will go away is by going to God and have faith that He will heal us. We must cry out to Him and allow Him to speak into our lives and obey Him.

It made me realize that I had been escaping the same way… by fanaticizing over another man. Our fantasy world is fun, exciting, romantic, and can be incredibly intoxicating. We don't realize that our spouses don't even stand a chance to compete with these fantasies, and that is incredibly unfair to them. The truth is that these fantasies and books never portray life as it really is. The reality is that our relationships can be difficult, depressing, frustrating, messy, hurtful, and sometimes harmful. But these relationships can also include great joy, celebration, romance, and friendship. I often laugh to myself when I think of Rick Warren when he chided, "Of course that person at the office looks attractive. You are seeing them when they are looking and acting their best. You don't see them in the bathroom with diarrhea, or vomiting, so of course, they are going to look more attractive than your mate." That hits home, doesn't it? We've all seen our spouses look their worst, have bad breath in the morning, and have slept next to their loud snores. But that is life. And life is worth living and feeling all that comes with it: joy, celebration, bumps, bruises, and pain. I think if we didn't have pain, we wouldn't be able to recognize the great blessing in life. Pain should be looked at as a gift.

Some people are born with rare genetic disorders where they are not able to feel any physical pain. Think about how dangerous this can be. They could burn or cut themselves and not even know it. They could be hit in the head and not realize that they may have a concussion. Physical pain is what stops us from getting hurt any further and to seek medical attention. Emotional pain should be what motivates us to seek spiritual attention and healing that can only come from God. We've got to stop escaping from it. It's been shown in studies that when we choose to escape, we are actually causing ourselves to become even more depressed.

If you look on the internet, and type in "ways to escape reality," you'll find several articles endorsing the notion of "escaping," and then list ways to accomplish it. The authors of these articles, of course, think that they are helpful to others. But we shouldn't look at escaping as a good thing. It's detrimental, because there is usually an underlying reason why we want to escape that needs to be addressed. Watching TV, reading a book, or being on the internet are not inherently bad. The problem arises when we feel we NEED to escape. The only way that pain will go away is by going to God and have faith that He will heal us. We must cry out to Him and allow Him to speak into our lives and obey Him.

Just how are we escaping? Here's a general list of some of the ways Americans are escaping (See below):

If you find yourself doing any of these activities excessively, you may need to ask yourself why you feel the need to escape. Ask God to show you the reason if you don't know off-hand, and then pray that God will deliver you from whatever may be causing you to escape. Choose to face your life and your circumstances. Choose to be present with the people around you and engage in life. Choose to work on mending the relationships that may have caused you to want to escape. Have someone help keep you accountable and make the necessary changes to remove any of these temptations. This may include putting your device, book, or other escape method away during the evenings

171

(or whenever you feel the temptation) so that you are not tempted to use them.

(Please read Appendix A for the statistics behind each of these areas)

<u>Video Games</u>
<u>Pornography</u>
<u>Excessive Internet Use</u>
<u>Excessive Social Media Use</u>
<u>Over or Under Eating</u>
<u>Reading</u>
<u>Travel</u>
<u>Medications</u>
<u>Alcohol</u>
<u>Illegal Drugs</u>
<u>TV & Movies</u>
<u>Listening to Music</u>
<u>Fantasizing or Daydreaming</u>
<u>Shopping</u>
<u>Gambling</u>
<u>Over-Working</u>
<u>Video games</u>

O nce we have received our initial healing, we need to make a habit of always using these methods to keep us from digressing back into our old, unhealthy habits of dealing with our pain. These habits can also be taught to our other family members, friends and kids. I once heard that even very young children can use these methods and heal them from pain that they may have experienced. Think about how transformational this would be. Instead of the pain popping back up again and again throughout their lives, they could take care of it right then and there. It would not follow them into their adult lives. They could then pass these methods on to their kids. Little by little, we could begin to heal this nation one generation at a time.

Perhaps a good way of making sure that we don't relapse back into our old ways is to create a "Monthly Emotional Health Calendar." On this calendar, we could set aside time during the month to create time for:

1. A daily time with God reading scripture, repenting, praying and then giving God time to speak to us.
2. A weekly, bi-weekly or monthly sin inventory and repentance.*
3. A monthly grieving inventory.*

4. A weekly, bi-weekly or monthly time to be alone with God to bring to Him our negative emotions and for Him to reveal to us the lies that we have believed and for Him to replace those lies with His truth.*
5. Slowly begin replacing time spent watching TV with spending time with our spouse, family and friends.
6. Making a daily habit of forgiving and saying you're sorry to those around you.
7. Schedule a weekly time to get together with your spouse to air any grievances, frustrations or hurt that you've felt this week. Try to come to a resolution. If you can't, then agree to come together again at a later date or time to discuss the issue once you both have spent time in pray for direction. Also give positive feedback on what went well throughout the week and include things that you have appreciated about your spouse.

So, instead of procrastinating, take the time right now to get your calendar out and schedule these important practices into your life. It's ok. Put this book down and do it. I'll wait!

Remember, it takes about six weeks to form a habit, so keep at it at least that long. Keep a journal with you during these times to record what God has been showing you, insights that you've gained and how your mood and/or relationships have changed because of these practices. Once you see a positive progression in your emotional health in your relationships with those around you, you'll be more likely to keep it up.

---

* These items can be combined into a once-a-month, 1-2 hour time alone with God.

PHASE FOUR SUMMARY AND DISCUSSION QUESTIONS

PHASE FOUR SUMMARY:

O = Allowing God the Opportunity to heal you
- Learning how we grieved in bible times and how to let go of grief today.
- Learning how to talk with God and then allowing Him to heal our emotional pain.
- Why we choose to escape and how we can heal our marriages.
- How to continue in freedom by setting up an emotional healthy calendar.

DISCUSSION QUESTIONS:

1. What did you learn about grieving? In what ways has our society rejected grieving? How can we improve how we grieve? Why is this important?

2. Have you ever experienced God healing your emotional pain? If so, please share your experience. If not, why do you think you haven't?

3. What do you think of the stories of "Listening to God" that the author shared? Do you think God can do the same for you? Why or why not?

4. Do you think by experiencing "Listening to God" with God, you would be able to experience emotional healing as well?

5. Do you ever find yourself escaping? If so, what method do you typically use to escape? What are some reason why escaping could be good or bad?

6. Based on the chapter on escaping and marriage, what are some ways in which we can improve our marriages?

7. Have you set up an emotionally healthy calendar? Do you think this would be helpful?

8. Have you experienced anything in this chapter so far that has helped you become more emotionally healthy? If so, please share your experience.

PRAYER TIME:

Ask God to help you process any grieving that you may need to release.

If you haven't experienced God while going through the steps of "Listening to God," then ask God to help you to hear His voice.

If you are escaping in some way, ask God to show you why you are escaping and to help you to overcome it.

Ask God to help you in your marriage by showing you how it can be improved.

PHASE 5: WORLD IMPACT

Helping Those Around Us Become Emotionally Healthy

v. **CHAPTER 14** | LIVING LIFE AS IT WAS MEANT TO BE

O nce we have truly been healed from our past wounds, have eliminated our fears, released our grievances, and have confessed to and have repented of our sins, we can then focus on what God has next for us. God has in mind a specific direction for our lives that He'd love for us to experience. He has called us to look past ourselves and see where we can best use the gifts, talents and personality that God has given us to accomplish His will. If we don't continue in fellowship with God and keep the communication with Him open, we may fall prey to living our lives in the safe, mundane and common routine life that most people experience. There will probably be many times in our life when we are to just find any job we are able to get in order to provide for our families and pay our bills. This is honorable. I know many men that especially feel the weight of that responsibility. But in time, as we have grown in our relationship with God, we should be asking God what He wants us to do with our lives. After all, He is the one who has designed and hardwired us, and who knows what we were created to do. I do believe that God can use us regardless of what we do for a living, or what stage of life we may be in, but I also believe that God's plan and desire for us is infinitely more than what we could ever hope to imagine on our own. I think our lives would be much more fulfilling, interesting and content if we were to always follow what God intended for us to do.

There are many resources available to help you to recognize what areas of work God may have created you to do. We have a few books at our house that we have referred to often to help guide us into the path that God has intended for us. One of those books is called, *Do What You Are: Discover the Perfect Career for You Through the Secrets of Personality Type*, by Paul & Barbara Tieger. I have to say that this book is very accurate at identifying your personality and associating jobs that go best with those personality traits. Another book that I really love, and have taught these concepts to others, is *S.H.A.P.E.: Finding & Fulfilling Your Unique Purpose for Life* by Erik Rees. The Acronym stands for Spiritual Gifts, Heart, Abilities, Personality and Experiences. I really like how this book helps you examine multiple areas of your life and have you think through the areas you feel God is calling you to use your gifts. Another book that I have enjoyed and would recommend is *Living the Life You Were Meant to Live*, by Tom Peterson.

So, for example, when I took the personality test from *Do What You Are*, I had discovered that my personality type is best suited for Interior Design as well as Ministry (pretty good fit, huh?), but when finding out my Spiritual gifts, I discovered that I have the gifts of teaching and of discernment. So, when I was teaching Interior Design at a local community college and ministering to students in need, I truly felt as though that job was meant for me. However, now that I am no longer teaching Interior Design, God has now called me into ministry by writing this book. I am still using my technical drafting skills (Experience) at my full-time job at local RV manufacturer, but God is still using me at church as well as with writing this book. However,

I would love to be able to be in ministry full-time, speaking to others about these concepts. I often think about that day while I'm waiting for my dream to be fulfilled.

Have you ever experienced a time in your life when you know that you've been right where God wanted you to be and were doing what God intended you to do? If so, what was it like? If not, why?

A friend of mine is a missionary doctor in Nepal. She could have chosen to begin a life of medicine helping people here in the United States and become "successful" and "wealthy" by our standards today. However, she was obedient to God calling her to become a doctor in Nepal. Her hospital is in such a remote area, that each time she goes back to Nepal, she has donkeys carry her supply of medicine to her hospital in which she serves. She doesn't deal with the ailments that doctors here do. She's treating those who have snake bites, are far into labor, are extremely sick, and who have grown huge tumors. She carries only the basic supplies and has limited medicine. Her hospital has electricity only part of the time. One time, she even had to kill a snake that was going into her bathroom! And believe it or not, every person in Nepal has a cell phone, even high up on the mountains!

Periodically she and a group of her friends and family will travel to the most remote part of Nepal and bring medical supplies and people along with her that will pray for those they encounter. Her mom and dad, who is also a doctor, have taken these trips with her. Being a Hindu nation, they believe in karma and reincarnation. The people of Nepal have no word for "Thank you," because they believe that everyone gets exactly what they deserve. Sometimes she has helped others see the God that she serves so devotedly and sometimes they choose not to. Yet, she is living a meaningful, fulfilling and sometimes exhausting life. I love talking with her because she loves to talk about the true important things in life. She has never been married or had kids, but her life is full. Her love for God is so evident. She has even memorized large portions of scripture. She thinks of God's word and His love for her when she looks at Mount Everest. How incredibly cool is that!

I know most of us can't just go and live in Nepal or go to some other third world country. But I do know that God has a plan for each of us. When I decided to no longer live with my feet in both Christian and non-Christian worlds and become truly devoted to God, my biggest fear was that God would have me become a missionary. I was just finishing college, and I just didn't want all that tuition money, time and effort of my Interior Design degree to go to waste. But, I prayed, "God, if it's your will, I'll go." But do you know what? God had already known about my Interior Design degree and chose to use it. God has used me in each of my jobs that have all involved Interior Design. There were times in my life that I have taken jobs to help support my family, when I know I was not using my gifts that God has given me. It can be frustrating and can become a period of waiting and longing for something better. In those periods, God can still use us. We can use our gifts at church by serving in areas of our interest and as well as in areas that need help. Did you know that in the average church, just 20% of the congregation does 80% of the work? Can you see the huge gap? Decide today to take on the responsibility of serving your part, and don't let the others become burnt out.

Because I am so passionate about us all doing what God has called us to do, I think it's especially important for us to keep this in mind for our kids. We need to encourage them in whatever interest they may have and support them in their extracurricular activities. Take them to the library and have them explore books on all kinds of opportunities of work. Let them hear stories of missionaries. Travel so that they can see different parts of the world (or watch videos on traveling to different destinations). Pray with them often so that they can begin a habit of praying for others, as well as seeking God's direction for their lives. Begin praying not only for their future spouse, but that God would lead them into the path that He has created for them. I know it's difficult to let go of our kids. We want to be close to our kids and grandkids and be able to see them often. But, for the sake of their contentment in life, and for their calling that God has for them, we sometimes will need to let them go. Then it will become our responsibility to visit them and to encourage them in whatever God has called them to do.

v. **CHAPTER 15** | HEALING THE NEXT GENERATION

O ne of the most eye-opening experiences in my life was when our family decided to become foster parents. There was a young girl at our church that was in foster care. We were told that her parents had given up their parental rights for her. After some time of prayer and much discussion, we decided that we wanted to adopt her. In order for us to adopt her, we needed to go through the foster care system and become foster parents. After many months of going through training, mounds of paper-work and fixing up our home to meet the requirements the foster care agency wanted, we were told just two days shy of her coming to our home that another family had taken her in instead. Since that family wanted to adopt her as well as her two brothers, that family was given priority. We were heartbroken. A few weeks later the foster care agency asked if we would be open to becoming foster parents for other children, so we decided to give it a shot.

While we were in the foster care system, my eyes were opened to just how bad our society has become. Each child had already experienced an enormous amount of pain. You would think that a child who is just 3 years old wouldn't have enough time to be affected and altered by their families, but they were. We once took in a family of three just during the week of Christmas break. They were 3, 5 and 7 years of age. The reason they were in temporary foster care was because the mother had stabbed the father in his leg. These kids never had a salad before, didn't know their right from left, and were uncontrollable. The middle boy would bang his head against the wall at night and would pee in his bed. The kids were so loud and active that I actually shut down emotionally. I could not take care of them. Fortunately (for me anyway) my husband was able to step in, and just a day or two later the mom was able to get her kids back.

We also took in a boy in his teens who wouldn't eat or talk with us. We then cared for a young girl that had been cutting herself on numerous occasions before she came to us. After that, we took in an older teenage girl whose mother would leave her and her siblings for weeks at a time by themselves. When she came to us, she had ten people that she would meet with on a regular basis (which was a part-time job in of itself making sure she got to all of her appointments) to help her overcome her emotional problems. This included a professional counselor, a psychiatrist, a CASA worker, a life-skills coach, her foster-care representative, and someone she could call if she was feeling anxious. I can tell you first-hand that in the short time that we cared for her, none of these professionals had helped her. She was (and still is) a damaged and emotionally immature young adult who is now living with her boyfriend several states away. She has a difficult time keeping a job, gets hurt frequently, and is a wreck emotionally. When she left our home, we decided to no longer be a part of the foster care system. It was just too emo-tionally draining for our family. I cared for each kid that we took in, but each of these kids were so emotionally damaged, it was difficult to see a bright future for them. The foster care agency that we were involved with did not endorse taking the kids to church unless the kids themselves chose to participate. How sad. They did not understand that God is the only one who can heal their pain.

After reading about another school shooting this week, I am again saddened at the general state of today's youth. Since college, God has put in my heart a special place for teens because I thought that if I would have had someone take notice of me when I was in high school and had discipled me, perhaps my life would have been very different. I had made a lot of poor choices while I was in high school, and I wanted to keep others from doing the same.

Early in our marriage, my husband and I became youth leaders at our church which we led for over ten years. We had many wonderful discussions, fun activities and missions' trips with our youth group that we still talk about often. However, we also have a few regrets. One of those regrets that we have is that we didn't talk about how to defend our faith, especially when it came to the topic of evolution. We have seen a few of our students fall away from their faith once they entered college because they were not prepared to defend the biblical view of creation. Since then, our family has watched the Genesis Science Network often and have learned a great deal about this issue, and just how much evidence there is on creation vs. evolution. I really wished we would have learned this material and discussed this with our students during those years. I would encourage you to do the same.

Another regret that I have is that we didn't provide an opportunity for our students to share the deep hardships they were facing. We always took prayer requests but didn't provide a time for our students to express their emotional needs that they had, or the harder struggles they were facing. I think sometimes we as adults think that kids don't face many difficult challenges in their life since most don't have a job or kids of themselves to support. However, as we now know from all of the school shootings that have happened during the last few years, that is not the case. In fact, I think students have a more difficult time sorting out and finding solutions to their problems that they face than we do. A friend of my son, who is in 9th grade, has stated that she has found herself escaping into her fantasy world that she has created since she was in 3rd grade. It began when other kids bullied and made fun of her. Her parents had divorced soon after, and she has been hurting ever since. Escaping is her way of coping from the life that she has, and unfortunately, she is not alone.

While finding out information about escaping, I came across an article that someone had posted on this topic. The article stated that escapism had now become common with young adults. What surprised me about this article was the response that followed. Many that responded were, in fact, young adults. However, many stated that they had been escaping since they were in grade school. Most of the responding posts were very sad. One response stated that escaping was better than committing suicide. Many others described their lives as being lonely, phony, and painful. My heart breaks for them. I wish they could experience all that God had originally intended for them. I wish that they could ask God the lies they have believed and then renew their minds with the truth. I wish that they can all find a loving Christian friend who can walk beside and support them.

I wish they can all find a good church where they can learn about God and become a part of a Christian community.

In many cases our youth today are not getting the emotional healing that they desperately need, even within the church. Churches usually teach bible stories (which should be called history), discuss current teen topics, and focus on having fun. But they should also be providing an opportunity for them to share what is really going on in their lives, and not just be given two minutes to blurt out a prayer request. They should be providing a conducive atmosphere in which they will feel free to share their deepest and darkest hurts, fears and sins with people they can trust.

Just think of the difference it would make if all of us could just focus on one or two kids to help guide them in their journey through life. Perhaps invite one of your kid's friend over whose parents work a lot, or who you know has a difficult home life. Take them to church with you. Let them see how you live and interact with one another. I think sometimes when we grow up in a dysfunctional home, we really don't ever learn what a healthy home should look like. So it's important for kids to see an emotionally healthy environment that they may never experience otherwise, so that hopefully they can decide to live a better life than what they had growing up. If you see a kid in your Sunday school class who you think may have some emotional issues, take them aside and ask them about their lives. Watch out for, pray for and encourage them often. Don't let them fall into the cracks that will lead them into making poor decisions. Encourage emotionally healthier kids to do the same. Encourage them to become role models to the struggling students that surround them. All it takes is one person affecting another, and that person affecting another, and the cycle to continue to create change and healing so that the inner pain that our children are facing doesn't continue. If we don't, we will continue to see more school shootings, suicides, and more hurt kids who then pass the pain along to their children.

V. **CHAPTER 16** | GIVING BACK

B
rennan Manning, the author and former priest who spoke
so well on God's love, has stated, "Do you honestly believe that with all the wrong turns you've made in your
past, the mistakes, the detours, the moments of sin, selfishness,
dishonesty, and degraded love, that God has used them all to
bring where you are today?" If you don't believe Manning's
statement, you should, because it's true. God has all kinds of
ways to use the terrible things in our lives for His ultimate good.
Only God can do that. He brings new life after a devastating for-
est fire, a rainbow after a thunderstorm, a beautiful baby after
hard labor. He can use the most difficult tragedy that you've experienced to shape and mold you into who you are today and
then use you to encourage and heal others.

We long to be with others who understand what we are going
through. A divorced woman can help and give comfort to another divorced woman. Those who have survived cancer can be
an encouragement to those with cancer. Those who have lost a
child can say the most healing words to those who are experiencing the same tragic loss. Others without common experiences
can sympathize and pray for us, but it's just not the same as getting encouragement from someone who has walked in your
shoes, has made it to the other side, and has discovered God's
goodness in the midst of the trial. We all need hope. Hope is
what gets us to that other side. It's the light at the end of the

tunnel. And even if the outcome isn't as we'd like it to be, we can still experience hope.

When my husband and I were trying to conceive for over five years, it was tempting to let go of hope. One day, while I was crying out to God over my frustration of not being able to conceive, God whispered to me the word "Hope." So, I decided to make my password at work to include the word "Hope" in it, so that I had to literally type it out each day and be reminded of the hope that I knew God wanted me to have. We did eventually have two beautiful boys, who are now teenagers. To this day, I still use the word hope in my password at work to remind me of God's goodness. I think it is very important to hold on to hope. It is a very important aspect to have. Without hope, we have the potential to fall into depression. It may be hard to see hope while we walk through a difficult time. That is why it is so important to seek God and to remember how He has answered our prayers in our past, and how He has given hope to those in the Bible, so that we can hold onto hope as we go through our suffering. It may be difficult to see hope while we walk through a hard time, but once we are on the other side of our suffering, we can then give hope to others who can't seem to find it. Not a false hope that everything will turn out how they want it to, but a sense of peace and expectancy that God can use the situation for His glory and our good. He always does. We just need to choose to look for the ways in which He does.

According to Larry Crabb, in his book, *Encouragement*, the ideal church should consist of people who are encouraging one another on a consistent basis.[1] He believes that counseling shouldn't be looked at as a profession, like a dentist or doctor with just one person with that job title, but as something we can all do for each other, with the goal of ministry in mind. Being a pastor's wife for over four years, I never realized before then how difficult it can be these days to be a pastor. There are those within the congregation who hardly speak to the pastor or share any of their most difficult circumstances, when they really should. But there are many more within the congregation that go to their pastor with many of life's issues, regardless of how small or large the problem is. This can be so overwhelming and has resulted in many burnt-out pastors. Counseling and encouraging should be the role of the entire church (which should include some form of training) in order to minister to, nurture, and love everyone effectively. Rick Warren's Saddleback Church, located in California, has recently begun offering classes in church counseling to their congregation. On their website it states, "This is a 30-week training class designed to help you learn a biblical paradigm through which you can help yourself and others to improve communication skills, discover the marriage God intends, develop a biblical foundation for parenting, or deal with grief, loss, anger, bitterness, inner personal struggles, or spiritual discouragement." I wish every church would offer such a class!

Even if you haven't gone through the same hurt as someone else, you can still encourage them. This is a trait that we've somehow lost over the years, so it's good to mention how we can encourage each other as God has intended. Instead of going to church hoping to connect with another person that we can tell our problems to, we should go to church with the mindset of ministry. Look for the chance to help others. The opportunities are there—you just need to pay close attention to those around you. There will always be some who wear their heart on their sleeve, but most people don't just blurt out their problems. Usually there are only small clues to indicate that something is bothering them. If you were to ask someone how they were doing, and they said, "Fine, under the circumstances," that's a ministry opportunity. Respond by asking the person an open-ended question (not a simple yes or no question) and try to find out what is bothering them. If you don't already know what this person may be referring to, you may ask, "So, what does "under the circumstances" mean? Is there something that happened? Tell me about it." Usually people are giving you clues to see if you are listening to them and if you care enough about them to ask about their situation.

I've noticed through the years, that people tend to talk one-sided. They talk, and you listen. Or you talk, and they listen. We are no longer asking the other person questions or wanting to take the focus off ourselves. Conversations should be like a game of volleyball—an equal back-and-forth between the two individuals. Sometimes people do need to "vent," but this may not end up being beneficial to their spiritual health. A true friend will listen, then ask questions for further understanding, then ask their friend how they can help, or pray for them right then and there. A person once told me that it really bothers them when people say, "I'll pray for you," and then walk away. Take advantage of the situation and pray for them at that moment, if at all possible. Just by taking that extra, immediate step, you'll help the other person feel more cared for. If there's not time to talk, ask if you can meet for coffee (or tea in my case), or for dinner. Give the person time to share their story.

Sometimes, however, you'll meet people that will remain one-sided during a conversation and really only want to talk about themselves. In time, inner healing may take away some of these tendencies, but what do you do until then? This is the approach that I have taken: View all people as ministry opportunities. A ministry is when you help others and do not expect anything in return for yourself (but don't let them monopolize your time either). God has put that person in front of you for a reason and that includes being a help to them, if at all possible. Once relationships grow, they may turn into friendships where there is truly a back-and-forth conversation, but for now, be content with where the relationship is at the moment.

Think about all of the loneliness, suicides, broken relationships, and wrong decisions or actions that might have been avoided if the person responsible for these problems were able to speak to a Christian who cared about them and were able to pray for them and give Godly advice BEFORE the situation began, or BEFORE it got worse. Instead, we usually find out about tragedies AFTER they've happened. How sad. I'm so tired of hearing about how a couple has filed for divorce, when I didn't even know they had any issues to begin with, or how a teen ran away before we knew about there being any problems at home. This has got to stop and we, as the church, must find ways help others to share what is really going on inside their homes and for us, the church, to provide that safe place for that to happen without condemnation.

I think one of the most personally healing things we can do is to help others. It helps us to take our eyes off ourselves and our situation by focusing on someone else and their needs instead of ours. Sometimes it can bring a joy that can't be gained by doing anything for ourselves. It can become something we can look back on in our lives with a great sense of satisfaction. But when we help others, we should do it without wanting anything in return. We shouldn't get upset with those around us if we don't receive a "thank you" or any recognition for our help. The joy is in seeing those around us become healed, not in the recognition it may bring or in a false idea of them being indebted to us.

Here are some verses to remind us of the importance of helping others:

- "Carry each other's burdens, and in this way you will fulfill the law of Christ" (Gal 6:2).
- "My command is this: Love each other as I have loved you" (John 15:12).
- "Each of you should look not only to your own interests, but also to the interests of others" (Phil. 2:4).
- "We who are strong ought to bear with the failings of the weak and not to please ourselves" (Romans 15:1).
- "We love because He first loved us. If anyone says, 'I love God,' yet hates his brother, he is a liar. For anyone who does not love his brother, whom they have seen, cannot love God, whom he has not seen" (1 John 4:1).

CHAPTER 17 | HEALING OUR NATION

*"If my people, who are called by my name, will
humble themselves and pray and seek my face
and turn from their wicked ways, then I will
hear from heaven and I will forgive their sin
and will heal their land" (2 Chronicles 7:14).*

A ccording to this verse, the best way to heal our land is for
all of us to humble ourselves and to repent of our sins.
It's easy to see that our society has declined, but it's a
little harder to pinpoint exactly what has happened throughout
the years, or what sins we have committed that have caused it. I
believe one of the largest ways we have sinned as a society is
that we are no longer following God or seeking His guidance.
Many have left the church. I blame both the church and individuals as to why. One article entitled, "Why Millennials are leaving church" by Rachel Held Evan (CNN) stated,

> ...young adults perceive evangelical Christianity to
> be too political, too exclusive, old-fashioned, un-
> concerned with social justice and hostile to lesbian,
> gay, bisexual and transgender people.
>
> I point to research that shows young evangelicals
> often feel they have to choose between their intel-
> lectual integrity and their faith, between science
> and Christianity, between compassion and holi-
> ness.
>
> I talk about how the evangelical obsession with sex
> can make Christian living seem like little more than
> sticking to a list of rules, and how millennials long

for faith communities in which they are safe asking tough questions and wrestling with doubt.[1]

She believes that most churches think that if they just had "edgier music, more casual services, a coffee shop in the fellowship hall, a pastor who wears skinny jeans, and an updated web site that includes online giving," that it will draw the twenty-something crowd back into the church. Those things may help, but what this generation wants is for us to be authentic. They can see right through us if they detect that we are performing. They want to see us talk about our struggles and how God has helped us through them. They want to see us display authentic faith and love for one another. They want to see us answer the tough questions about sex, gender identity, and creation vs evolution. They want to see us caring about our community and social justice issues. They want to see us loving the GLBT community.

I can't say that I disagree with any of those desires, even though I am way past the "millennial" age. I am also yearning for those things. I want to have those type of conversations with the younger generation. I want to invite my GLBT friends to church and know that they will be welcomed and loved *(Much more about this subject in my next book).* I want to see people, including the pastor, be honest about their temptations, fears and pain, so that I don't feel like I am "less of a Christian" because I struggle when it appears that others aren't. I want to see lives transformed. I want to see caring eyes when others look at me. I want to experience God in every area of my life and for others to want that too. I want to see the church as it was meant to be.

Another article entitled, "Church-goers tend to be happier people" by Stephanie Pappas, stated, "Religious people are more satisfied with their lives than nonbelievers, but a new study finds it's not a relationship with God that makes the devout happy. Instead, the satisfaction boost may be from closer ties to earthly neighbors." What that statement is telling me is that those of us who are going to church, are doing so because of the relationships we've built with others who are attending, but it isn't necessarily because of a growing deeper relationship with God. People are feeling loved by people, but not God. They are not experiencing Him. How incredibly sad is that!? Hopefully these people are at least experiencing God on their own, but they should also be experiencing God at church. If you're not, then why go to church? Please don't get me wrong. I really love fellowshipping with those around me at church. It truly brightens my day and it does help me feel more loved, but it is because of my relationship with God that I want to see them and share with them what God has done and is doing in my life!

I have attended a church before where I can honestly say that I had never sensed the Holy Spirit during a normal service at any time during a year of attending there. When I mentioned this to the pastor, he just had a look on his face, like "Oh yeah, the Holy Spirit. We forgot about Him!" As I have stated before, our churches need to be both scripturally and Holy Spirit led. We need to always be learning more about God and His ways from scripture, be challenged to grow in our faith and feel God's presence. I know this seems like a tall order to ask for from our pastors. Perhaps it is. But this is something we should expect from our local church. If we are not experiencing those things, then we need to first look at ourselves and ask ourselves why we aren't. It could be that we are the ones who either not are paying attention, or don't really have a desire or will to grow or are not seeking out an experience with God.

Another way we have sinned is through our relationships. Instead of working on our marriages, we are divorcing. Instead of working on our relationships at work, we just quit our jobs. Instead of working on our relationships with our families, we become estranged. Instead of working on our relationships with those who might have hurt us at church, we just stop going. When will it end? Why do we no longer want to do the work to repair the relationships of those around us?

I believe that we no longer know how to live in community as God intended. We have become so separate and so individualistic, that we have lost our ability to live with our neighbors, friends, and relatives well. I live in Goshen, Indiana, and I see the people of the Amish faith all around me. I think they might be one of the last groups of individuals in our generation to experience community as it was meant to be. They worship, shop, go to school, and work all in the same vicinity with one another. They have churches and schools, located every few miles, and they all seem to know each other well.

The one thing that I most admire about the Amish is that they are there for one another during times of hardship. They don't have insurance, but when there is a fire and a house is in need to be rebuilt, they pull their money together and spend a few days rebuilding their neighbor's house. When money needs to be raised for an illness, or loss of work, they have a "haystack" dinner or breakfast and raise funds.

When researching how Americans typically spend their time, I was surprised to find out that the average time spent on socializing during a week day is only about a half hour. On weekends it's about an hour. In contrast, we usually are spending about 2.7 hours a day watching TV. That means that we'd rather watch TV than socialize. I work for an RV company that hires many of the Amish. The Amish just can't understand why an RV would need three TV's. That does kind of seem unnecessary, doesn't it? I don't know why we Americans love our TV so much. I love watching TV. It is relaxing and entertaining. However, when we are not spending adequate time communicating with our spouse, kids, friends and family, we run the risk of our relationships becoming strained. All relationships need time to develop and nurture.

Dr. James Dobson has stated that he figured a good minimum goal to spend with our spouse should be: an average of 15–30 minutes a day, a two-hour time span talking sometime during the week or weekend, 1 night out a quarter, and one weekend away a year. This is time spent talking…not while you are watching TV or looking at your cell phone.

We also need additional time for our kids. Of course, our little ones need a lot of our time and attention. That is necessary. However, when our kids become a little older and become more independent, I am noticing teenagers that are suffering from their parents not spending enough time with them. "The one key instance," said Melissa Milkie, a sociologist at the University of Toronto, "found where the quantity of time parents spend does indeed matter is during adolescence: The more time a teen spends engaged with their mother, the fewer instances of delinquent behavior. And the more time teens spend with both their parents together in family time, such as during meals, the less likely they are to abuse drugs and alcohol and engage in other risky or illegal behavior. They also achieve higher math scores. The study found positive associations for teens who spent an average of six hours a week engaged in family time with the parents. "So these are not huge amounts of time…" Milkie said.

However, adolescents who were spending time with their stressed-out or abusive parent had the opposite effect. Kevin works as a teacher for the Crossing in South Bend, a Christian based high school for kids that have been kicked out of the public-school system. Many of the teens come from a difficult home life… usually with one parent, who may possibly be on drugs, who is abusive, or who just aren't home much. These kids are looking for a role model… someone who will spend time with them and give them guidance. Kevin takes these teenagers to job sites where they learn basic construction skills. One teenager, who recently moved away, told Kevin that he thought of him as a Dad. How sad to think that Kevin has only known this teenager for just a few months, but of all of the male role models he has come a crossed throughout his life, he only considered Kevin as a father figure. It doesn't take a huge time commitment to make a difference in someone's life. The point is, we need to spend quality time with our kids. They need to know that we are there for them and that we care about what is going on in their lives, by asking them open-ended (not yes or no) questions. Ask them what the best and worst part of their day was. Ask them if they have any upcoming quizzes or tests. Ask them anything! Sometimes, to help us out with this, we have purchased a deck of cards that have conversation starters on them. If you can't think of what to ask them, use something fun like that as a tool to get your teenager to open up their lives with you. Do fun things together as a family. Build up your bank of fun memories with them by taking vacations. You don't need to spend a lot of money to have fun together. You just need to be creative.

Another way to restore relationships is to become quick at saying "we're sorry." Think about how many relationships would be restored, if everyone said it to those they have offended. One of my favorite movies of all time (and one of the best artistically drawn animations), is "Tale of Despereaux." It's a story about a young mouse who wanted to learn about bravery, honor and truth. Born in a world where it is only acceptable to be timid, the main character, Despereaux Tilling, becomes an unlikely hero. The story begins in a small village where the royal kitchen creates a soup each year that the whole town is able to enjoy. One year, there was a rat who loved soup who wanted to get a closer look at the new creation. As the rat climbed up the castle wall to get a good smell, he fell into the soup. The queen, while taking her first sip of the soup, sees the rat, has a heart attack and dies to the horror of the king, princess and the entire village. The narrator states, "When something hurts this much, there must be a reason. There must be someone to blame." So, the king blamed the rats and they became banned from the town. Soup was no longer served. The town grew gray and gloomy. There was no more rain. The princess was forbidden to leave her room. "However, the princess had hope. And with hope, you are never anyone's prisoner," because she knew her prince would rescue her one day. Despereaux had been reading an exciting book about courage, honor and decency. He learned how to become a gentleman. The rat had tried to tell the princess that he was sorry for what he had done, but the princess became afraid of him instead. This angered the rat, so he decided to make the princess pay by tying her up and allow the cat to attack her. Despereaux heard the princess's plea for help and then rescued her and became her hero.

It's a wonderful story, but what chokes me up every time I watch it is when the town becomes renewed when one person after another begins to say, "I'm sorry." The rat said he was sorry to the princess, the princess said she was sorry to the rat. A jailer told his daughter he was sorry for giving her up. Tears were shed and hearts where healed. The sun came out again. Soup was served, and the townspeople rejoiced. The narrator then states, "A single act of forgiveness can change everything," and the town was truly restored.

The first step to real change and healing the relationships around you is admitting what you have done wrong. If someone comes to you and tells you that you have hurt them in some way, or if you realize that you have hurt someone, you need admit what you have done wrong in that situation. You cannot change what you cannot see, so it's important to be able to see why it hurt the other person. Don't wait for the other person to begin this step. You can begin the healing process by first taking responsibility for your part of the conflict. You should not hide, lie, become defensive, minimize or blame someone else for what you have done. This only creates more hurt because when you don't take responsibility and admit your fault, you are not acknowledging that the other person has a right to their feelings, and that is destructive and hurtful.

The second step is to say that you are sorry for what you did. That in of itself would mend many broken relationships. However, confessing and saying you're sorry is different than actual repentance. Repentance requires change. When it comes to saying we're sorry, we need to make sure we are saying it with the intention of not hurting that person again in the same way. There should be a commitment to change. When someone repeatedly does something to hurt someone over and over, their "I'm sorry" falls flat. Sorry doesn't mean anything at that point unless that person has made a commitment to change.

The third step is to create a community that can surround you and keep you accountable. You need others around you to encourage you, to check up on you to see how you are doing in that area and to pray for you. You should be willing to accept honest feedback from those around you for you to see your progression in that area of conflict.

Step four is about consequences. You should set up steps that would take place if there is no effort to change. This should help motivate you to not only change, but to begin to change quickly. This also helps to provide a way for the other person to help keep you accountable. You should always envision what may happen if you choose to continue in the bad behavior. Keep in mind that divorce should always never be used as a consequence, unless there is physical, or emotional abuse taking place (in which case you should seek the help of law enforcement immediately to provide you with safety). Your spouse needs to understand that you will stick by them no matter what.

We need to learn the act of forgiving others daily and always say that we're sorry to those we have hurt. I believe that with these two acts alone, our homes, communities and our nation (and our world!) can become healed. We need to let go of our pride and of our defenses. We need to allow God to give us the inner strength to face our hurting relationships and do the hard work that it will take to restore them. We need to stop, as Rick Warren states, "paying too much attention to people's words and not enough to their feelings." There have been times when those closest to me have hurt me deeply by the words they have spoken to me. Those words then become like a recording, playing them over and over in my head (which is what the devil wants me to do). When we forget to look at the feelings behind the words, we are not looking not at the real issue. The real issue is that those words are coming from someone who is hurting. And we have the power to stop that hurt, with God's help, if we only choose to do so. Being right is not important. Restoring the relationship is. I once heard a quote that stated, "God does not demand of me that I accomplish great things. God does demand in me that I strive for excellence in my relationships." Let's live our lives with that goal always on our mind.

PHASE FIVE SUMMARY AND DISCUSSION QUESTIONS

PHASE FIVE SUMMARY:

W = <u>World</u> Impact.
- Finding out what our calling in life is.
- How to help our kids become emotionally healthy.
- How to help others around us become emotionally healthy.
- How to heal our land by restoring our relationships and our churches.

DISCUSSION QUESTIONS:

1. Have you taken any of the personality tests that were mentioned in this phase of the book? If so, what was the result? What do you feel your calling in life is? What are your spiritual gifts? How do you think you could use those gifts to help others?

2. Do you think you are at a point in emotional healing that you could begin to help others grown in that area as well? Why or why not?

3. How do you think you could help the kids that are around you grow more emotionally healthy?

4. How do you think you could help others in your life grow more emotionally mature?

5. What are some things that you've learned from this book? What lessons will you be incorporating into your life?

PRAYER TIME:

Thank God for all that He has done with helping you emotionally while reading this book. Then ask God to help you to continue to grow emotionally healthy in all areas of your life.

Ask God to help you find an accountability partner (if you haven't already) to confess to and to discuss your emotional and spiritual health with.

Ask God who in your life you can share this information with who needs emotional healing, and then pray for an opportunity to help them to grow emotionally healthy.

CONCLUSION

I believe that if we apply what we've learned to allow God to heal us emotionally and then use what we've learned to help those around us, this nation (and then this world!) will become stronger, healthier and more truly devoted to God. I'm convinced of it! Please join God and me in this journey! Feel free to share this information to others.

We can remember each of the steps we've taken through this book, by thinking of the word A.L.L.O.W. and what each letter stands for:

Phase 1: A = <u>Admitting</u> you are unhealthy
1. We need to first admit that we are, in fact, messed up.
2. Learning what happens when we don't let go of pain.
3. Learning how we initially became unhealthy will help us learn how to avoid being unhealthy in the future.
4. Learning how the devil works so that we can defeat him.

Phase 2: L = Replacing <u>Lies</u> with the Truth
1. Why memorizing scripture is important.
2. Understanding how much God loves us will help heal us.
3. Learning to trust in God's character.
4. How to take every thought captive.

Phase 3: L = <u>Letting Go</u>
1. Confronting your fear of healing.
2. Learning why prayer is important and why we need to make it become a larger part of our lives.
3. Confessing your sins, and learning about generational sin.

Phase 4: O = Allowing God the <u>Opportunity</u> to heal you

1. Learning how we grieved in bible times and how to let go of grief today.
2. Learning how to talk with God and then allowing Him to heal our emotional pain.
3. Why we choose to escape and how we can heal our marriages.
4. How to continue in freedom by setting up an emotional healthy calendar.

Phase 5: W = <u>World</u> Impact.

1. Finding out what our calling in life is.
2. How to help our kids become emotionally healthy.
3. How to help others around us become emotionally healthy.
4. How to heal our land by restoring our relationships and our churches.

Let me hear from you!

If you have found the information in this book helpful, or if you would like me to come speak at your local church or conference, please contact me through my email below:

Rhonda Mitschelen
Email: mitschelenr@gmail.com

FAITH BUILDING MINISTRIES

APPENDICES

Video Games

A study appearing in the medical journal Pediatrics, conducted by research scientist Douglas A. Gentile, Ph.D., examined video game usage rates of 3,034 children and teenagers. Video game addiction statistics from this study revealed the following:

- The average length of time spent playing video games was 20 hours per week
- An estimated 72 percent of American households play video games
- An estimated nine percent of the 3,034 participants in the study showed signs of video game addiction
- Four percent of percent of study participants were categorized as extreme users who played video games 50 hours per week on average
- According to a Springer Link research study, video game addiction statistics show as much as 40 percent of online video game players admitted to playing online games as a way to escape from the real world.

(Alarming Video Game Addiction Statistics n.d.)

Pornography

- **Every second**, $3,075.64 is spent on pornography
- 28,258 people are viewing pornography every second.
- Every 39 minutes, a new pornographic video is created in the United States.

- $13.33 Billion was spent in the porn industry in 2006. U.S. porn revenue exceeds the combined revenues of ABC, CBS and NBC.
- 1000.000 websites offer illegal child pornography.
- The average age of the first internet porn exposure is age 11.
- There are 4.2 million pornographic websites (12% of total websites)
- 42.7% of internet users view pornography.
- 1 in 7 youths have received sexual solicitation.

(Internet Pornography Statistics 2014)

Excessive Internet use

- Every fourth child is addicted to the internet
- According to the study, which we first saw on Motherboard, researchers estimate that 6% of the world's population is addicted to the internet.
- The world's population is roughly 7 billion people, so that makes for about 420 million people addicted to the internet.

(Kosoff 2014)

Are you wondering why anyone would become addicted to a computer?

It seems that there are various reasons for people to turn to the computer and to become addicted but the most logical explanation is that people use the computer to escape reality or to cover up their emotions. Many find it easier to socialize from behind closed doors in an online fantasy world. Others think that if they shop or gamble excessively online that nobody else will notice. Regardless of the reason why an individual may be using the computer excessively, there are consequences that result and in some cases the need for treatment to overcome this addiction is absolutely necessary.

Many people use the computer to self-medicate for some other problem such as because they are anxious in certain situations such as in social situations or because they are depressed. Others will turn to the computer to hunt for information and then realize that they just can't get enough information. Still others may use the computer as a means of distracting them from the real world or from emotional situations that they have experienced.

https://www.addictions.com/computer/computer-addiction-statistics-that-may-surprise-you/

(Computer Addiction Statistics That May Surprise You n.d.) Studies from the University of Iowa show that Internet addiction is quite common among males ages 20 to 30 years old who are suffering from depression.

Excessive Social Media Use

Social Networking and Marital Unhappiness

In one study, researchers from Boston and Santiago, Chile, looked at the relationship between social networking and marital happiness, as well as trends linking social network availability and divorce rates. They focused on 1,160 married couples between the ages of 18 and 39 who were surveyed by the University of Texas at Austin's Population Research Center. These couples were asked to rate their relationship on a 10-point scale based on statements such as:

- We have a good relationship.
- My relationship with my partner is very healthy.

The researchers also measured the extent to which partners in these relationships utilized social networking sites such as Facebook, Twitter, and MySpace. Here is what they reported: Increased use of social networking is correlated with poorer marital happiness and a higher likelihood of a troubled relationship, along with thoughts of divorce.

This still doesn't answer the question of which comes *first*—an unhappy <u>marriage</u> or greater use of social networking? Aren't those men and women who are unhappy just turning to social media as an outlet for their unhappiness? Maybe, but maybe not. Let's look a little further.

Social Networking and Divorce
This same research team looked at how growth in the use of social networking might be related to divorce rates. To do this they determined the "penetration rates" of sites such as Facebook across the U.S. over time—specifically, from 2008 through 2010. What they discovered was something that family lawyers had been reporting anecdotally for some time: The greater penetration of social media from 2008 to 2010 was positively correlated with increases in divorce rates.

Taken together, the above results constitute evidence suggesting that excessive use of social networking and similar sites could indeed not just play a role in compensating for an unhappy relationship but may actually *contribute* to that unhappiness.
https://www.psychologytoday.com/blog/the-almost-effect/201405/can-excessive-social-networking-harm-marriages
(Nowinski 2014)

Eating

According to data from the National Health and Nutrition Examination Survey (NHANES), 2013–2014[2,3,4,5]

- More than 1 in 3 adults were considered to be overweight.
- More than 2 in 3 adults were considered to be overweight or have obesity.

- More than 1 in 3 adults were considered to have obesity.
- About 1 in 13 adults were considered to have extreme obesity.
- About 1 in 6 children and adolescents ages 2 to 19 were considered to have obesity.

Consequences of Obesity

People who have obesity, compared to those with a normal or healthy weight, are at increased risk for many serious diseases and health conditions, including the following:[5,6,7]

- All-causes of death (mortality)
- High blood pressure (Hypertension)
- High LDL cholesterol, low HDL cholesterol, or high levels of triglycerides (Dyslipidemia)
- Type 2 diabetes
- Coronary heart disease
- Stroke
- Gallbladder disease
- Osteoarthritis (a breakdown of cartilage and bone within a joint)
- Sleep apnea and breathing problems
- Some cancers (endometrial, breast, colon, kidney, gallbladder, and liver)
- Low quality of life
- Mental illness such as clinical depression, anxiety, and other mental disorders[8,9]

National Estimated Costs of Obesity
- The medical care costs of obesity in the United States are high. In 2008 dollars, these costs were estimated to be $147 billion.[15]

(Adult Obesity Causes & Consequences 2018)

Reading Romance Novels

These statistics offer insights to help you understand this billion-dollar-a-year industry.

- **Romance novels are a $1.4 billion industry, dwarfing the literary book market by millions.**
- Romance novel share of the U.S. fiction market: 34% (source: Nielsen BookScan/PubTrack Digital 2015)
- Who is the romance book buyer? (source: Nielsen Books & Consumer Tracker)
  - Female: 84%
  - Male: 16%
- Age of the romance book buyer: 30–44 years old

(Nielsen Books & Consumers 2015)

Traveling

The travel and tourism industry is one of the world's largest industries with a global economic contribution (direct, indirect and induced) of over 7.6 trillion U.S. dollars in 2016.

By <u>Nicole Melancon</u>

Like most travel bloggers, I have been completely shocked by the tragic news of the death of fellow travel blogger Anita Mac. Anita Mac, the vibrant face behind the popular travel blog Travel Destination Bucket List, took her own life.

Oftentimes, the life of a world traveler appears to be glamorous and enviable on the outside. Their amazing stories of traveling the world are full of adventure, travel and beautiful photos from surreal places. Their lives seem so wonderful and happy and fun. Yet what is said to the outside world may be completely different than what is really happening inside. On the outside they may seem to have it all, but on the inside they may be falling apart, bleeding, hurting, and suffering in silence.

Although I never met Anita, for some reason the news of her suicide has made me think deeply about the real reasons behind why we travel. Of course, there are many reasons why we travel. We travel to relax, to have fun, to experience adventure, to see the world, to spend time with family and friends and to get away from it all. Yet have we ever taken a hard look at the real reasons we are traveling sometimes? Have we ever realized that sometimes we are using travel too much as an escape, to the point where it can become dangerous?

Throughout my life, I will admit that I have been guilty of using travel as an escape during hard times. Most likely we all have to some degree. So what is it we are exactly trying to escape? Unfortunately, our lives. We want an escape from the daily grind of a life of routine. Escape from the devastation of a broken heart or major disappointment. Escape from things we don't want to necessarily face back at home like a serious illness, a death, a divorce, or a layoff. Escape from something we cannot change.

Travel is an escape. The further you go off the beaten path, the easier it is to forget. Yet traveling for the wrong reasons and not facing your demons in your life can be dangerous. You always have to come home at the end of a trip. Although you may forget about your struggles and pain while you're having the time of your life half way around the world, it is important to have a good, happy place to come back to. An inner peace with your life at home and on the road.

People may never know why such a young, vibrant woman who appeared to have it all took her own life. Yet her tragic passing has been an eye-opening experience for many to take a look at their own lives and happiness. I know it has for me.

Follow Nicole Melancon on Twitter: www.twitter.com/@third-eyemom

(Melancon n.d.)

Medications

Prescription drug abuse IS STILL DRUG ABUSE. Get the facts:

- More than 1,600 teens begin abusing prescription drugs each day.
- Many kids mistakenly believe prescription drugs are safer to abuse than illegal street drugs.
- After marijuana and alcohol, the most common drugs teens are misuing or abusing are prescription medications.
- 12–17 year olds abuse prescription drugs more than ecstasy, heroin, crack/cocaine and methamphetamines combined.
- Two-thirds of people 12 and older (68%) who have abused prescription pain relievers within the past year say they got them from a friend or relative.[1]
- The most commonly abused prescription drugs are pain medications, sleeping pills, anti-anxiety medications and stimulants (used to treat attention deficit/hyperactivity disorders).
- Almost 1 in every 4 teens in America say they have misused or abused a prescription drug.
- One in five teens (20%) who have abused prescription drugs did so before the age of 14.
- 9% of teens in a recent study reported using prescription pain relievers not prescribed for them in the past year, and 5% (1 in 20) reported doing so in the past month.

(Rx Safety Matters n.d.)

Illegal Drugs and Alcohol

Addiction is more common than many realize. There were approximately 20.6 million people in the United States over the age of 12 with an addiction in 2011.

Although most people don't get the treatment they need, over 3 million people in 2011 received treatment for their addiction.

- Percent of persons aged 12 years and over with any illicit drug use in the past month: 10.1% (2015)
- Percent of persons aged 12 years and over with any non-medical use of a psychotherapeutic drug in the past month: 2.4% (2015)
- Over 20 million Americans over the age of 12 have an addiction (excluding tobacco).
- 100 people die every day from drug overdoses. This rate has tripled in the past 20 years.
- Over 5 million emergency room visits in 2011 were drug related.
- 2.6 million people with addictions have a dependence on both alcohol and illicit drugs.
- 9.4 million people in 2011 reported driving under the influence of illicit drugs.
- 6.8 million people with an addiction have a mental illness.
- Rates of illicit drug use is highest among those aged 18 to 25.
- Over 90% of those with an addiction began drinking, smoking or using illicit drugs before the age of 18.

(CDC 2017)

Alcohol Statistics

Alcoholism is one of the most common addictions affecting Americans. It also an addiction that goes untreated in many cases because of the legality of the substance. However, the recorded rates of alcoholism are decreasing (18.1 million people in 2002 to 16.7 million in 2011), but the addiction is still a cause for concern.

- Binge drinking is more common in men; 9.1% of men 12 and older reported heavy drinking 5 or more days in a month, while 2.6% of women reported this.
- Over 11% of Americans have driven under the influence.
- Out of 16.6 million people with alcoholism, 2.6 million were also dependent on an illicit substance.
- It is estimated that over 95% of those who need treatment for alcoholism do not feel they need treatment.
- More people receive treatment for alcohol than any other substance.

TV & Movie

In today's world, television is the main source of entertainment. What effect is this having on society, especially for children and young people? And what will it mean when they become adults?
If you have ever driven through a neighborhood at night, you have probably noticed a familiar blue glow emanating from the windows of houses. You can picture the scene inside: As the centerpiece of the room, the television has captured the complete attention of those assembled before it. Whether it is an individual, a couple or an entire family, all eyes are fixed on this modern invention with its endless barrage of images.

The Radio Corporation of America started manufacturing color television sets on March 25, 1954, at its Bloomington, Indiana plant, helping to usher in "the wonderful world of color." Since that time, the number of households with TVs has steadily risen. According to the U.S. Census Bureau, the number of homes with television sets increased from 87% in 1960 to over 98% in 2001. Most homes have more than one (2.4 per home on average), totaling 248 million in the U.S. alone—and most today do not remember a time without television.

The Plug-in Drug

For some, watching television consumes their entire day. This is especially true of older Americans, who watch more TV (97%) than any other age group. Those living alone or who are shut-ins often find this activity the only way to endure long lonely days.

In fact, it is projected that in 2004, the average adult will spend 1,669 hours watching television. that is the equivalent of 70 days a year—well over 4,900 days in the average lifespan! Put another way, over 13 years of the average person's life will be spent in front of the television. No wonder it is often referred to as the "plug-in drug."

Is "TV addiction" a real phenomenon? It may well be. Notice this February 23, 2002 article published by *scientificamerican.com*: "Among life's more embarrassing moments have been countless occasions when I am engaged in conversation in a room while a TV set is on, and I cannot for the life of me stop from periodically glancing over to the screen. This occurs not only during dull conversations but during reasonably interesting ones just as well" ("Television Addiction Is No Mere Metaphor").

Indeed, many have experienced this exact sensation of being drawn to the TV. Turn a TV on and conversation and physical activities stop. Before you know it, the entire day has disappeared.

According to the same article, "The term 'TV addiction' is imprecise and laden with value judgments, but it captures the essence of a very real phenomenon. Psychologists and psychiatrists formally define substance dependence as a disorder characterized by criteria that include spending a great deal of time using the substance; using it more often than one intends; thinking about reducing use or making repeated unsuccessful efforts to reduce use; giving up important social, family or occupational activities to use it; and reporting withdrawal symptoms when one stops using it.

"All these criteria can apply to people who watch a lot of television. That does not mean that watching television, per se, is problematic. Television can teach and amuse; it can reach aesthetic heights; it can provide much needed distraction and escape. The difficulty arises when people strongly sense that they ought not to watch as much as they do and yet find themselves strangely unable to reduce their viewing. Some knowledge of how the medium exerts its pull may help heavy viewers gain better control over their lives."

But does this really mean that people are addicted to television? The article continues: "To some researchers, the most convincing parallel between TV and addictive drugs is that people experience withdrawal symptoms when they cut back on viewing. Nearly 40 years ago, Gary A. Steiner of the University of Chicago collected fascinating individual accounts of families whose set had broken—this back in the days when households generally had only one set: 'The family walked around like a chicken without a head.' 'It was terrible. We did nothing...Children bothered me, and my nerves were on edge. Tried to interest them in games, but impossible. TV is part of them.'"

For some, life without television is truly unbearable. How important is it? A story out of the southwestern Florida city of Fort Myers relates how a 17-year-old boy was charged by police with soliciting to commit murder. The boy was willing to pay $2,000 to have his mother killed, but with one stipulation: "Make it look like a robbery, but don't damage the TV!"

The Babysitter

In this hectic world, in which it seems there are always a million things that need to be done, many desperate parents resort to television as a babysitter. After all, it's always available any time of the day or night. It never complains and never needs to be paid. And best of all, it keeps the child amused and completely engrossed.

But is this "babysitter" a harmless electronic device? What effect does it have on children? And what kind of patterns are developing in them?

A recently released study holds some answers. *Zero to Six: Electronic Media in the Lives of Infants, Toddlers and Preschoolers*, published by the *Kaiser Family Foundation*, provides a look into the use of media among the very young and their parents. Some of its findings include:

- 80% of children use screen media, whether TV, movies or video games.
- 77% turn the television on by themselves.
- Two-thirds request a particular program or surf channels using a remote.
- 65% live in homes in which the TV is on half the time or more.
- 36% live in homes in which the TV is *always* on (considered a "heavy" TV household).
- In "heavy" TV households, 77% of children watch it every day.
- They are also less likely to read (59% vs. 68%).
- They are less likely to be able to read at all (34% of children ages 4–6 from heavy TV households can read, compared to 56% of others the same age).
- The majority of parents (59%) say their 4-to-6-year-old boys imitate aggressive behavior seen on TV.
- 30% of children under 2 have a TV in their bedroom.

Remember, these statistics are merely for infants to six-year-olds!

The Effects on Kids

There is much debate on whether and how viewing television influences children in their formative years. But the mounting evidence from numerous studies indicates that there are real adverse affects. For example: There is a direct correlation between time in front of a TV and the rise of obesity in children. This sedentary time, often accompanied with consuming high-calorie and high-fat junk foods, replaces time that could have been spent engaging in energy-burning activities.
Consider the following:

• Number of medical studies since 1985 linking excessive television watching to increasing rates of obesity: 12
• Percentage of American children ages 6 to 11 who were seriously overweight in 1963: 4.5%; in 1993: 14%
• Number of ads aired for "junk-food" during four hours of Saturday morning cartoons: 202

(The Real Truth n.d.)

Music

In a development which confirms what many of us perhaps knew all along, research has shown that listening to music all the time as a teenager turns you into a doleful depressive (or alternatively that being a doleful depressive teenager makes you listen to music all the time). Youngsters who read, by contrast, tend to be in tiptop mental health.

Other forms of media—movies, TV etc.—have no particular effect, according to Dr Brian Primack, medicine prof at Pittsburgh uni. But music listening is strongly linked to major depression, one of the most serious mental conditions, while reading is associated with a mind in the pink.

"At this point, it is not clear whether depressed people begin to listen to more music to escape, or whether listening to large amounts of music can lead to depression, or both. Either way, these findings may help clinicians and parents recognize links between media and depression," says Dr Primack.

"It also is important that reading was associated with less likelihood of depression. This is worth emphasizing because overall in the US, reading books is decreasing, while nearly all other forms of media use are increasing."

According to a statement issued yesterday by Pittsburgh Univ.:

The study involved 106 adolescent participants, 46 of whom were diagnosed with major depressive disorder...
The researchers found that young people who were exposed to the most music, compared to those who listened to music the least, were 8.3 times more likely to be depressed. However, compared to those with the least time exposed to books, those who read books the most were one-tenth as likely to be depressed. The other media exposures were not significantly associated with depression.

It seems that if your teenage offspring spend their time listening to less-fancied genres of music they may yet avoid depression. The study authors report that "major depressive disorder is positively associated with *popular* music exposure" (our emphasis).

(Page 2011)

Daydreaming or Fantasizing

Snap out of it! That daydream you're having about eloping to the Bahamas with Johnny Depp or Angelina Jolie is leaching away your happiness. In a new global study, researchers used iPhones to gauge the mental state of more than 2000 volunteers several times a day—even when they were having sex. The results indicate that, if you want to stay cheerful, you're better off focusing on the present, no matter how unpleasant it is.

The human mind is remarkably good at straying from the moment. That ability allows us to remember the past, plan for the future, and "even imagine things that never occur at all," says Matthew Killingsworth, a doctoral student in psychology at Harvard University. "As a scientist, it's something I do all the time."

But is daydreaming good for us? That's a tough question to answer, says Killingsworth. To find out, scientists must survey subjects several times a day to record their mood and activities at that exact moment. "People are quite good at telling you how happy they are right now," he says, "but less at telling you how happy they were last week." In the past, researchers have used buzzing pagers, which reminded volunteers to write in a diary, or they bought their subjects expensive mobile devices like Palm Pilots. Both methods are hard to scale up. So Killingsworth, a former product developer at a Cambridge, Massachusetts, software company, took advantage of something thousands of people already have and use all the time: iPhones.

In 2009, Killingsworth and Harvard psychologist Daniel Gilbert, with the help of a friend who is a software engineer, launched a study on a Web site called Track Your Happiness.org. After answering basic questions about their age, location, and general satisfaction with their job, marriage, or car, iPhone owners could sign up to receive one or more text messages a day. These texts nudged them to visit an online survey to report how happy they were feeling and pick from 22 different choices, including shopping, watching television, or working, to describe what they were doing right then. Subjects also recorded whether they were thinking about that activity or about something else that was pleasant, neutral, or unpleasant.

Although the study was only advertised on Killingsworth's Web site, he soon had nearly 5000 subjects from 83 different countries sending in data several times a day. The volunteers were surprisingly diligent, responding, on average, to about 83 percent of the nudges...

When the researchers analyzed the experiences of a subset of 2250 adults, about three-quarters of them from the United States, the first thing they noticed was just how often people weren't thinking about what they were doing. Over all, subjects' minds were wandering about 47% of the time, the duo reports online today in *Science*. Only during sex did mind-wandering occur less than 30% of the time.

The daydreaming was not good for people's moods: Volunteers were unhappier when their thoughts were elsewhere. Statistical tests showed that mind-wandering earlier in the day correlated with a poorer mood later in the day, but not vice versa, suggesting that unhappiness with their current activity wasn't prompting people to mentally escape. Instead, their wandering minds were the cause of their gloom. Mental drifting was a downer for subjects during even the dullest activities, like cleaning, the researchers found. "I'm sure there are some situations where mind-wandering can be helpful," says Killingsworth. But based on these results, those "are probably pretty rare."

The findings "challenge the foundations of psychology," says Lisa Feldman Barrett, a psychologist and neuroscientist at Northeastern University in Boston, who pioneered data gathering with Palm Pilots. Psychologists assume that the mind responds to a stimulus out in the world, but in this study, "it almost looks like the stimulus is irrelevant."

Still, says Barrett, the study has limitations. For one, not everyone can afford to own an iPhone, so the study sample may not be representative of the population. And as to whether mind-wandering was really the cause of subjects' unhappiness, Barrett would like to see stronger evidence. Killingsworth's statistical analysis "is a good start, but not a sufficient answer," she says. He showed a cause-and-effect relationship for samples that were several hours apart from each other, Barrett notes, but that says little about "shifts in consciousness [that] occur on the order of milliseconds."

(Schenkman 2010)

Shopping

WRITTEN *BY* JOSHUA BECKER ·

There is little disagreement that shopping comprises a significant portion of our lives. And to some extent, this is entirely expected—to live is to consume. However, in most developed nations, shopping has long since passed the role of necessity and has entered the realm of sport.

Our fascination with shopping and consumption has produced many harmful effects on our lives (debt, stress, and busyness). And yet, it continues. Unfortunately, to a degree that few us even realize.

Based on a variety of studies and research methods, here are 17 staggering statistics that articulate our current passion and obsession for shopping:

1. The average woman makes 301 trips to the store annually, spending close to 400 hours a year shopping. This amounts to 8.5 years spent shopping during a typical lifespan. (**NY Daily News**)
2. Americans spend more on shoes, jewelry, and watches ($100 billion) than on higher education. (**Psychology Today**)
3. Shopping malls outnumber high schools in America. (**Affluenza**)
4. 33% of Americans shop online at least once per week. 69% shop online at least monthly. (**Mintel**)
5. While 50% of online shoppers will increase the size of their orders just to hit the free shipping minimum. (**Mintel**)

6. An estimated two-thirds of the U.S. gross domestic product (GDP) comes from retail consumption. (**The Balance**).
7. On average, an American between the ages of 18 and 65 has $4,717 of credit card debt. (**TIME**)
8. 63% of Americans do not have enough savings to cover a $500 emergency. (**Forbes**)
9. When asked about hobbies, girls (age 13–18) identified shopping as their favorite pastime. (**Adweek**)
10. And 96% of adults and 95% of teens admit they participate in some form of retail therapy. (**Yahoo**)
11. More than a third of adults and teens said shopping made them feel better than working out. (**Yahoo**)
12. The average American throws away 65 pounds of clothing per year. (**Huffington Post**)
13. The $8 billion home organization industry has more than doubled in size since the early 2000's—growing at a staggering rate of 10% each year. (**Uppercase**)
14. Americans now spend more money on dining out than groceries. (**Fox News**)
15. The average American women spends 190 hours each year shopping for clothes, shoes, or window shopping. That same survey found that these same women spend 95 hours shopping for food—this task occupies only half the time of shoe, clothes and window shopping. (**Forbes**)
16. 50% of Americans will go shopping on Black Friday. (**Syracuse**)
17. Worldwide, total retail sales were more than $22 trillion in 2014, according to a report from eMarketer.com. And total annual U.S. retail sales have increased an average of 4.5% between 1993 and 2015, according to the U.S. (**The Balance**)

The numbers paint a jarring picture of excessive shopping and unnecessary consumption. This fascination with shopping might be okay if it was improving the happiness of our lives. But as most of us know, the happiness derived from accumulating material possessions doesn't last. We ought to be looking elsewhere.

(Becker n.d.)

Gambling

Even without the physical triggers so commonly associated with drug addiction, gambling disorders can wreak just as much havoc in a person's life. While drug addiction works as a substance-based disorder, gambling addictions have more to do with a lack of impulse control, according to the U.S. National Library of Medicine.

Ultimately, it's the loss of control that defines addictive behavior regardless of the substance or activity involved. Gambling addiction statistics present this "loss of control" factor in a stark and alarming light.

Gambling addiction statistics show how problem gambling can up-end a person's life in more ways than one. Not unlike other types of addiction, people most susceptible to gambling also suffer from other disorders of which they may or may not be aware.

Probably the most glaring revelation to be had from gambling addiction statistics lies in the consequences that result when gambling disorders go untreated.

1. Gambling Trends

As with all types of data, certain trends or patterns of behavior start to surface within a given population. Gambling addiction statistics are no different. According to the University of New York, some of the more prevalent gambling trends show:

- The likelihood of developing a gambling addiction increases 23-fold for people affected by alcohol use disorders
- Over 80 percent of American adults gamble on a yearly basis
- Three to five gamblers out of every hundred struggles with a gambling problem
- As many as 750,000 young people, ages 14 to 21 has a gambling addiction

2. Gambling & Criminal Activity

As far as gambling and criminal activity goes, gambling addiction statistics reveal a direct correlation between the severity of a gambling addiction and the likelihood of committing crimes. According to Georgia State University, rates of gambling addiction for criminal offenders far exceed rates found among non-offenders. On average, an estimated 50 percent of those affected by gambling problems commit crimes in order to support their addiction.

3. College Gambling

Gambling addiction statistics show people between the ages 20 and 30 have the highest rates of problem gambling. According to the University of North Carolina at Wilmington:
- 75 percent of college students report having gambled during the past year
- The risk of developing a gambling addiction more than doubles for young adults in college settings
- An estimated six percent of American college students struggles with gambling problems

4. Gambling & PTSD Trends

People affected by post-traumatic stress disorder or PTSD live with high levels of stress and anxiety on a daily basis. Gambling addiction statistics show high rates of gambling addiction among PTSD sufferers.

- PTSD symptoms affect anywhere from 12.5 to 29 percent of problem gamblers
- 34 percent of those who seek treatment for gambling addiction exhibit symptoms of PTSD

5. Gambling & Mental Illness

As addictions in general alter brain chemical functions in destructive ways, people struggling with gambling addiction have a higher likelihood of developing mental disorders. According to the University of North Carolina at Greensboro, gambling addiction statistics show a high incidence of certain types of mental illness, some of which include:

- Depression disorders
- Anxiety disorders
- Substance abuse disorders
- Anti-social personality disorder

As with any other type of addiction, a gambling addiction can only get worse when left untreated.

(Addictions.com n.d.)

Over-Working

There's no doubt that technology has simplified the way we carry out our day-to-day routines. Computers help us do things faster, emails and text messages let us always be in touch, and the internet makes it easy to find the answer to any question with just a quick Google search.

While being constantly plugged in can make us feel safe, connected, and in-the-know—both at work and at home—it also means we never *really* clock out.

It's one thing to pull a long day every once in a while to finish a project or deal with a crisis, but it's another to routinely stay late at the office or work into the night. That's chronic over-work—and it can have extremely negative impacts on your health, happiness, and overall quality of life.

But working overtime has become the norm for most people. It's one of those things everyone kinda knows is bad for us, but no one really listens. Trouble is, failure to prioritize a healthy balance isn't just bad for the employees—it's actually bad for employers, too. Read on to learn exactly why it's bad for our health *and* our performance at work, and who's to blame.

Why Overworking is Bad for Your Health

There are numerous research studies out there showing the overwork—and the resulting stress—can lead to all matter of health problems.

It impairs your sleep.

A wide body of research has shown that overwork can negatively impact your sleep—whether it's the resulting stress, the staring at the computer screen, or just not having enough time to unwind before hitting the hay. This can cause us to build up what's called "sleep debt," which is kind of like being over-drawn at a bank. Chronic sleep debt raises the risk of obesity, heart disease, stroke, and diabetes. In the short-term, lack of sleep can have significant effects on the hippocampus, an area of the brain involved in memory creation and consolidation.

The fact is, most of us get tired more easily than we think we do. Think you're one of those "lucky people" who can get by fine with only five or six hours of sleep? *The Wall Street Journal* reports that for every 100 people who think they're a member of this "sleepless elite," only five actually are. Only 1–3% of people can actually pull off sleeping five or six hours a night without their performance suffering

It gets in the way of good habits.

Working too much can take a toll on the body and brain in two main ways—by boosting stress and by getting in the way of exercise, healthy eating, and other good habits.

For example, when you're overtired, you rely more on caffeine to get you through the day, you tend to make unhealthy food choices and working out becomes a thing of the past. A study in the journal *Nature Communications* found that when people are overtired, healthy food choices tend to go out the window for two reasons. First, it slows activity in the areas of our brains responsible for ranking different foods based on what we want and need. Secondly, it causes an increase in the brain's amygdala, which is responsible for controlling the salience of food. Over time, poor food choices can lead to weight gain and even obesity.

It's really bad for your heart.

A long-running study of more than 10,000 civil servants in London found that white-collar workers who worked three or more hours longer than a normal, seven-hour day had a 60% higher risk of heart-related problems than white-collar workers who didn't work overtime. Examples of heart-related problems included death due to heart disease, non-fatal heart attacks, and angina, a condition caused by low blood supply to the heart.

A follow-up study of over 22,000 participants found that people who worked long hours were 40% more likely to suffer from coronary heart disease than those who worked standard hours.

What about overworking might be causing heart disease, specifically?

Research suggests that it might have something to do with your personality. In fact, the "Type A vs. Type B" personality test was originally aimed to determine how likely it was that a person would develop coronary heart disease. Considering Type A folks tend to be more competitive, tense, time-oriented, and stressed out—which is often intensified by overworking—their personality type is often associated with a higher risk.

It can cause heavy drinking.

In 2015, the Finnish Institute of Occupational Health published the largest ever study of the correlation between working patterns and alcohol consumption. In the study, a group of researchers put together a dataset of over 330,000 workers across 14 different countries.

They found that 48 hours of work per week was the magic number: When people worked more than 48 hours per week, they were more likely to engage in "increased risky alcohol use." Risky alcohol use was defined as more than 14 drinks per week for women and more than 21 drinks per week for men.

They also found that people who worked long hours were 11% more likely to be heavier drinkers than those who worked normal hours, regardless of gender.

It can lead to type 2 diabetes in low-income workers.

In 2015, a group of researchers investigated the role of long working hours as a risk factor for type 2 diabetes. They found that the link between longer working hours and type 2 diabetes is apparent in individuals in the low socioeconomic status groups. This was true regardless of age, sex, obesity, and physical activity, and remained even when they excluded shift workers from the analysis. Another study showed an association between long hours and type 2 diabetes in low-income workers.

Overall, these findings show how strong of a relationship a person's mental state can have on physical health.

Why Overworking is Bad for Business

If better health and happiness isn't enough of an incentive to do something about chronic overwork, it turns out overworking can have a legitimately negative impact on a business' bottom line. Sarah Green Carmichael of *Harvard Business Review* calls the story of overwork "the story of diminishing returns":

keep overworking, and you'll keep making avoidable mistakes and getting lost in the weeds—all while not actually producing more.

More input doesn't necessarily mean more output.

Do longer work hours equate to more work getting done? From time to time, yes—but not when "overtime" becomes "all the time."

Research by the Business Roundtable found employees saw short-term gains when they pushed their workweek to 60 or 70 hours for a few weeks at a time if, for example, they needed to meet a critical production deadline. But increasing the number of hours worked in the office from 40 to 60 hours doesn't result in more output: "In fact, the numbers may typically be something closer to 25–30% more work in 50% more time," writes Sara Robinson for Salon.

Why? Robinson explains that most people do their best work between hours two and six of working in a given day. By the end of an eight-hour day, their best work tends to be behind them—and by hour nine, fatigue begins to set in and productivity levels drop. They won't be able to deliver to their full potential—especially if they aren't invigorated by something like a rare, critical deadline—and they'll end the day completely exhausted.

Interestingly, one study out of Boston University's Questrom School of Business found that managers actually couldn't tell the difference between employees who actually worked 80 hours per week and those who just pretended to. What's more, managers tended to punish employees who were transparent about working less—but there was no evidence that those employees actually accomplished less, nor were there any signs that the overworking employees accomplished more.

You're more likely to make mistakes.

Speaking of exhaustion, researchers have found that overwork—and the resulting stress and exhaustion—can make it far more difficult to do everything that a modern office requires, including interpersonal communication, making judgment calls, reading people, or managing one's own emotional reactions.

You lose sight of the bigger picture.

Ever heard of the term "goal reactivation?" According to a 2011 study from the University of Illinois, people can easily lose focus and get lost in the weeds of a task or project if they work on it continuously without stopping.

The breaks we take to recharge, eat meals, or spend time with the people we love help us step back from our work and stay mindful of how our work contributes to our goals. The study cites that these things reliably contribute to overall better performance at work.

(Kolowich n.d.)

Bluemel, Craig. "The Origin of the English Word for God: Part One." *The Bible Answer Stand Ministry*. Accessed June 9, 2018. http://www.bibleanswerstand.org/God.htm.

Campanile, Carl. "1 in 5 City Preteens Have Mental Woes." *New York Post*. Last modified 2013. https://nypost.com/2013/03/25/1-in-5-city-preteens-have-mental-woes/.

Coffey, Tony. "Can Anything Good Come Out of Temptation? (Part Two)." *Bible Answers*. Last modified 2007. Accessed June 9, 2018. http://www.bibleanswers.ie/2007?view=archive&month=11.

Corsi, Jerome. "Psych Meds Linked to 90% of School Shootings." *WND*. Last modified 2012. Accessed June 9, 2018. https://www.wnd.com/2012/12/psych-meds-linked-to-90-of-school-shootings.

Crabb, Lawrence, and Dan Allender. *Encouragement*. Grand Rapids: Zondervan Publishing House, 1984.

Crone, Billy. *The Character of God*. Lexington: Get a Life Media, 2017.

Dawkins, Richard. *The Blind Watchmaker: Why the Evidence of Evolution Reveals a Universe without Design*. Norton & Company, Inc, 1986.

Held, Rachel. "Why Millennials Are Leaving the Church." *CNN*. Last modified 2013. Accessed June 9, 2018. http://religion.blogs.cnn.com/2013/07/27/why-millennials-are-leaving-the-church.

Holland, Kimberly, and Elsbeth Riley. "ADHD by the Numbers: Facts, Statistics, and You." *Healthline*. Accessed June 9, 2018. https://www.healthline.com/health/adhd/facts-statistics-infographic#demographics.

Ingraham, Christopher. "America's Top Fears: Public Speaking, Heights and Bugs." *Washington Post*. Last modified 2014. Accessed June 9, 2018.

https://www.washingtonpost.com/news/wonk/wp/2014/10/30/clowns-are-twice-as-scary-to-democrats-as-they-are-to-republicans/?utm_term=.076f0c95a926.

Keller, Tim. *The Prodigal Prophet: Jonah and the Mystery of God's Mercy*. New York: Viking, 2018.

Kupelian, David. *Snapping of the American Mind*, 2015.

MacDonald, William. *Believer's Bible Commentary: New Testament*. Nashville: Thomas Nelson Publishers, 1990.

Mangis, Michael. *Signature Sins*. Downers Grove: InterVarsity, 2008.

Murray, Christopher, Marie Ng, and Ali Mokdad. "The Vast Majority of American Adults Are Overweight or Obease, and Weight Is a Growing Problem among US Children." *The Institute for Health Metrics and Evaluation*. Accessed June 9, 2018. www.healthdata.org/news-release/vast-majority-american-adults-are-overweight-or-obese-and-weight-growing-problem-among.

Nicholson, E.F. "Millions Of People Feel The Need To Escape, But From What?" *Information Clearing House*. Last modified 2014. Accessed June 9, 2018. http://www.informationclearinghouse.info/article40272.htm.

Ortberg, John. "Flourish: Nobody's Perfect." In *Menlo Church*. Menlo Park, 2017.

Paxman, Lauren. "One in 12 Teenagers Self-Harm (but Most Grow out of It by Their Twenties)." *Daily Mail Online*. Last modified 2011. Accessed May 25, 2019. https://www.dailymail.co.uk/health/article-2062629/One-12-teenagers-self-harm-grow-twenties.html.

Strauss, Richard. "God Is So Good." In *The Joy of Knowing God*. Loizeaux Brothers, Inc., 1984.

Tennant, Agnieszka. "A Shrink Gets Stretched." *Christianity Today*. Last modified 2003. Accessed June 9, 2018. https://www.christianitytoday.com/ct/2003/may/7.52.html.

The National Domestic Violence Hotline. "Statistics." https://www.thehotline.org/resources/statistics/.

Thompson, Andrea. "Bad Memories Stick Better Than Good." *Live Science*. Last modified 2007. Accessed June 9, 2018. https://www.livescience.com/1827-bad-memories-stick-good.html.

Watson, Elwood. "Millennial Stress College Years and Beyond." *Diverse: Issues in Higher Education.* https://diverseeducation.com/article/51755.

Weber, Lauren, and Sue Shellenbarger. "Office Stress: Him vs. Hers." *Wall Street Journal*, May 5, 2013. https://www.wsj.com/articles/SB10001424127887324678604578340332290414820.

"Alcoholism and Alcohol Abuse." *New York Times*. Last modified 2013. http://www.nytimes.com/health/guides/disease/alcoholism/risk-factors.html.

Antidepressant Use in Persons Aged 12 and Over: United States, 2005–2008. NCHS Data Brief Number 76, 2011. https://www.cdc.gov/nchs/data/databriefs/db76.pdf.

"Facts: General Statistics (USA)." *Stop Suicide.* https://stopsuicide.info/facts/.

"How Do I Accept Jesus as My Savior?" *InTouch Ministries.* Accessed June 9, 2018. https://www.intouch.org/Read/content/how-do-i-accept-jesus-as-my-savior.

Illegal Drug Use. FastStats, 2017. Accessed June 9, 2018. https://www.cdc.gov/nchs/fastats/drug-use-illegal.htm.

"Mental Illness Basics." *MedicineNet.* Accessed June 9, 2018. https://www.medicinenet.com/mental_illness/article.htm#what_causes_mental_illness.

Preventing Suicide 2018 What Is Suicide?, 2018. https://www.cdc.gov/violenceprevention/pdf/suicide-factsheet.pdf.

"Sigmund Freud (1856 - 1939)." *UK Apologetics.* Accessed September 6, 2018. http://www.ukapologetics.net/22truthaboutfreud.html.

"The Life of Charles Darwin & Whether He Became a Christian." *Creation Worldview Ministries.* Accessed June 9, 2018. https://www.creationworldview.org/articles_view.asp?id=27.

NOTES

Introduction

[1] *Illegal Drug Use, FastStats*, 2017, accessed June 9, 2018, https://www.cdc.gov/nchs/fastats/drug-use-illegal.htm.

[2] *Antidepressant Use in Persons Aged 12 and Over: United States, 2005–2008, NCHS Data Brief Number 76*, 2011, https://www.cdc.gov/nchs/data/databriefs/db76.pdf.

[3] Lauren Paxman, "One in 12 Teenagers Self-Harm (but Most Grow out of It by Their Twenties)," *Daily Mail Online*, last modified 2011, accessed May 25, 2019, https://www.dailymail.co.uk/health/article-2062629/One-12-teenagers-self-harm-grow-twenties.html.

[4] Christopher Murray, Marie Ng, and Ali Mokdad, "The Vast Majority of American Adults Are Overweight or Obease, and Weight Is a Growing Problem among US Children," *The Institute for Health Metrics and Evaluation*, accessed June 9, 2018, www.healthdata.org/news-release/vast-majority-american-adults-are-overweight-or-obese-and-weight-growing-problem-among.

[5] Carl Campanile, "1 in 5 City Preteens Have Mental Woes," *New York Post*, last modified 2013, https://nypost.com/2013/03/25/1-in-5-city-preteens-have-mental-woes/.

[6] Paxman, "One in 12 Teenagers Self-Harm (but Most Grow out of It by Their Twenties)."

[7] Lauren Weber and Sue Shellenbarger, "Office Stress: Him vs. Hers," *Wall Street Journal*, May 5, 2013, https://www.wsj.com/articles/SB10001424127887324678604578340332290414820.

[8] Elwood Watson, "Millennial Stress College Years and Beyond," *Diverse: Issues in Higher Education*, https://diverseeducation.com/article/51755.

[9] "Alcoholism and Alcohol Abuse," *New York Times*, last modified 2013, http://www.nytimes.com/health/guides/disease/alcoholism/risk-factors.html.

[10] The National Domestic Violence Hotline, "Statistics," https://www.thehotline.org/resources/statistics/.

[11] *Preventing Suicide 2018 What Is Suicide?*, 2018, https://www.cdc.gov/violenceprevention/pdf/suicide-factsheet.pdf.

[12] "Facts: General Statistics (USA)," *Stop Suicide*, https://stopsuicide.info/facts/.

[13] David Kupelian, *Snapping of the American Mind*, 2015.

Chapter 1
[1] John Ortberg, "Flourish: Nobody's Perfect," in *Menlo Church* (Menlo Park, 2017).
[2] Lawrence Crabb and Dan Allender, *Encouragement* (Grand Rapids: Zondervan Publishing House, 1984).
[3] Richard Dawkins, *The Blind Watchmaker: Why the Evidence of Evolution Reveals a Universe without Design* (Norton & Company, Inc, 1986).
[4] "The Life of Charles Darwin & Whether He Became a Christian," *Creation Worldview Ministries*, accessed June 9, 2018, https://www.creationworldview.org/articles_view.asp?id=27.
[5] *Antidepressant Use in Persons Aged 12 and Over: United States, 2005–2008.*
[6] Kimberly Holland and Elsbeth Riley, "ADHD by the Numbers: Facts, Statistics, and You," *Healthline*, accessed June 9, 2018, https://www.healthline.com/health/adhd/facts-statistics-infographic#demographics.
[7] "Mental Illness Basics," *MedicineNet*, accessed June 9, 2018, https://www.medicinenet.com/mental_illness/article.htm#what_causes_mental_illness.
[8] Natural News, 3-8-17
[9] "How Do I Accept Jesus as My Savior?," *InTouch Ministries*, accessed June 9, 2018, https://www.intouch.org/Read/content/how-do-i-accept-jesus-as-my-savior.
[10] Jerome Corsi, "Psych Meds Linked to 90% of School Shootings," *WND*, last modified 2012, accessed June 9, 2018, https://www.wnd.com/2012/12/psych-meds-linked-to-90-of-school-shootings.
[11] Michael Mangis, *Signature Sins* (Downers Grove: InterVarsity, 2008).
Chapter 2
[1] Tim Keller, *The Prodigal Prophet: Jonah and the Mystery of God's Mercy* (New York: Viking, 2018).
[2] Agnieszka Tennant, "A Shrink Gets Stretched," *Christianity Today*, last modified 2003, accessed June 9, 2018, https://www.christianitytoday.com/ct/2003/may/7.52.html.
Chapter 5
[1] William MacDonald, *Believer's Bible Commentary: New Testament* (Nashville: Thomas Nelson Publishers, 1990).
[2] Billy Crone, *The Character of God* (Lexington: Get a Life Media, 2017).
[3] Craig Bluemel, "The Origin of the English Word for God: Part One," *The Bible Answer Stand Ministry*, accessed June 9, 2018, http://www.bibleanswerstand.org/God.htm.

[4] Richard Strauss, "God Is So Good," in *The Joy of Knowing God* (Loizeaux Brothers, Inc., 1984).

[5] "Sigmund Freud (1856 - 1939)," *UK Apologetics*, accessed September 6, 2018, http://www.ukapologetics.net/22truthaboutfreud.html.

[6] Prayer from www.InTouch.org.

Chapter 6

[1] MacDonald, *Believer's Bible Commentary: New Testament*.

Chapter 7

[1] Christopher Ingraham, "America's Top Fears: Public Speaking, Heights and Bugs," *Washington Post*, last modified 2014, accessed June 9, 2018, https://www.washingtonpost.com/news/wonk/wp/2014/10/30/clowns-are-twice-as-scary-to-democrats-as-they-are-to-republicans/?utm_term=.076f0c95a926.

Chapter 9

[1] Mangis, *Signature Sins*.

[2] Ibid.

[3] Tony Coffey, "Can Anything Good Come Out of Temptation? (Part Two)," *Bible Answers*, last modified 2007, accessed June 9, 2018, http://www.bibleanswers.ie/2007?view=archive&month=11.

[4] Crone, *The Character of God*.

Chapter 11

[1] Andrea Thompson, "Bad Memories Stick Better Than Good," *Live Science*, last modified 2007, accessed June 9, 2018, https://www.livescience.com/1827-bad-memories-stick-good.html.

Chapter 12

[1] E.F Nicholson, "Millions Of People Feel The Need To Escape, But From What?," *Information Clearing House*, last modified 2014, accessed June 9, 2018, http://www.informationclearinghouse.info/article40272.htm.

[2] Refer back to chapter nine for additional information on generational sin.

[1] Crabb and Allender, *Encouragement*.

Chapter 17

[1] Rachel Held, "Why Millennials Are Leaving the Church," *CNN*, last modified 2013, accessed June 9, 2018, http://religion.blogs.cnn.com/2013/07/27/why-millennials-are-leaving-the-church.

Made in the USA
Lexington, KY
16 June 2019